HOMESICK

ANGELA STEELE

with photographs by Tim Mercer

MERCER books

First published in 2025 by Mercer Books

MERCER books

www.mercerbooks.co.uk

ISBN 978-1-7391224-6-1

Copyright © Angela Steele

The right of Angela Steele to be identified as the author of this work has been asserted by her in accordance with the Copyright, Designs and Patents Act 1988.

Photographs Copyright © Tim Mercer

The right of Tim Mercer to be identified as the author of these works has been asserted by him in accordance with the Copyright, Designs and Patents Act 1988.

Design by Craig Stevens

All rights reserved. No part of this publication may be reproduced, stored in or introduced into a retrieval system, or transmitted, in any form, or by means (electronic, mechanical, photocopying, recording or otherwise) without the prior written permission of the publisher. Any person who does any unauthorised act in relation to this publication may be liable to criminal prosecution and civil claims for damages.

A CIP catalogue record for this book is available from The British Library

This book is sold subject to the condition that it shall not, by way of trade or otherwise, be lent, re-sold, hired out, or otherwise circulated without the publisher's prior consent in any form of binding or cover other than that in which it is published and without a similar condition including this condition being imposed on the subsequent purchaser.

Any flaws and inaccuracies that remain are the authors and the authors alone.

Only papers from certified sources are used and all ink is vegetable based

For Richard
who makes things possible

and to Ian K
who left us far too soon;

and to all the men
who, like them,
love unconditionally...

> "What do you want to do with your one wild and precious life?"
>
> MARY OLIVER. *THE SUMMER DAY.*

HOMESICK

Give sorrow words;
the grief that does not speak
knots up the o'er wrought heart
and bids it break.

WILLIAM SHAKESPEARE. *MACBETH*

HOMESICK

...something is still starved
and I cannot yet
recognise what it is...

....what the hunger is
what mineral, herb, nutrient, prayer, place
is missing...

...where lies the lack,
body, heart, mind, soul,
how to know?

...all that is known is
something is missing, hungering, thirsting, lacking,
starving even...

...hiraeth

> "If we have never been a stranger, that is because we have never left home."[1]
>
> BARBARA BROWN TAYLOR.

Please, come in. You are welcome here. Leave your baggage on the doorstep. You may pick it up on the way out. What you will find here is not about you and your set of beliefs but about me and mine. It is about a struggle to make sense of my faith, my culture, and my being here, on this planet now.

I struggle with what Jesus says to do and what Christianity actually does. I struggle with why we make such a fetish out of Jesus and forget the one who birthed him. I struggle with worshipping Jesus when all we were ever asked to do was follow him. I struggle, more than anything, with the notion that God is male; father, king and ruler. Constantine has a lot to answer for. If we are to be a people of salt and light as Jesus asks, then it follows that we are walkers of the Way. Jesus said, "I am the Way, the Truth and the Life", he didn't, ever, say "Worship me." Jesus was about love and longing; about truth and humility; about discomfort and desire and about joy and peace. But above all he was about revolution and revelation — and healing.

Jesus knew that salt seasons and preserves. We are life's seasoning and preservative. He knew that light shines and illuminates. Who are we not to shine and illuminate, not to pass on the light of Love to an unloved and unloving world? We are not asked to foist our brand of Christianity, our brand of faith on others — just to love them. We are not asked to lay our brand of democracy and cultural upbringing on others — just to walk with them. We are not to assume ours is the only way — we must be open and unafraid and hospitable to those who are strangers and aliens. And above all — we must listen.

Our God speaks. Our God speaks quietly, and the world is clamorous. The hardest thing to do is to get out of God's way. The best thing to do is to get out of God's way.

> 'There is a tide in the affairs of men* which taken at the flood leads on to fortune… On such a sea are we now afloat, and we must take the current when it serves, or lose our venture.
>
> JULIUS CAESAR.

(*William Shakespeare means 'mortals' or 'human beings' of course. The language is different now, *we* have no excuse…)

---

[1] *Holy Envy*. 2019. HarperOne New York

I write this book in all honesty. I am not seeking to destabilise your beliefs, your thinking, nor your practices. I do not seek to discredit your religion nor your culture or way of life. Why would I? I am a minister of religion and I gratefully acknowledge my debt to the denomination to which I belong. And here comes the but...

I am a tilter at windmills, a curious questioner, a chaser of hares. I look under rocks and in the sky. I seek meaning in streams and oceans. What does all that mean? I do not know. I only know that I have a compulsion to push boundaries, to challenge authority and reason with lie. And there is every possibility that I am wrong.

My eldest son once said to me, "Mummy, where are the clouds going?" I had no answer then and there are no easy answers now. I have only wonderment and curiosity and a deep love for the sacredness of all creation that leads me ever on, and I don't know where I am going. And the mistakes and failings are all mine. You make your own.

No books? said God. No books?!
There's two on your bookshelf I gave you
years ago.
Now is the time to find them and read.
No books indeed!

Go, get the one you picked up
and put back on the shelf
that one has many a treasure I have given you.
No books!

R.S. Thomas, St. John of the Cross
Emily Dickinson, Sue Monk Kidd,
Richard Rohr and Matthew Fox,
Macrina Wiederkehr, Lynn Anderson and
Thomas Merton.
Daniel O'Leary, Desmond Tutu and the Dali Lama,
Nicola Slee and Phyllis Tickle, Wendell Berry
and Mary Oliver.
Carola Moosbach.
And on and on and on.....
No books?

Hold out your hands
and I will give you books

Hands have held books
and time after time
book after book has
led further and further,
deeper and deeper into others' wisdom,
love and distress.

And therein I have found my own voice.

God has been made in the image of Man. God is Father, He, Himself. Man has made God in his own image. Man, and Mankind has limited God and hampered humankind's understanding by giving God male human form. The One whom Man names 'God' is better not named. The Source of our Being is not a noun but pure verb. An eternal, living, relationship of Love, energy moving between you and me and the One who breathed life into the universe in a single and continuous act of creative love.

'In the beginning was the Word and the Word was with God and the Word was God...'

And the Word was not just a Noun,
a thing, a Name.
The Word was a Being,
a Verb – an Energy,
a Thought, an Action, an Energy
a Doing, a Spark of Imagination.

In the beginning the Word,
was an Adjective
describing –
de-scribing the Work of God
Lover, Love, Loving,
Doer, Dancer, Dancing
Singer, Song, Melody.

In the beginning –
as it is now and always will be.

And we, we are the Word of God
made flesh.
Lovers, Loving,
Dancers, Dancing,
Singers of Life's Melody,
the Imagination of God.

'As it was in the beginning, so it shall be...'

In the beginning...

First there was Nothing
no thing

In the beginning there was silence
exploding into the void
sending shockwaves
of being into a formless shape
of cacophony and chaos.

And then there was Something
and in between the space between
Nothing and Something.

The Silence quietly came

In the single beat of a hummingbird's wing
in the indrawing and outhaling of a shrew's sigh,
in the time it takes for a bat's squeak
to earspeak

Something like a Whisper came

Breathed, came into the world to wrap
the noise and noisomeness in a cocoon
of dark velvet touching,
smoothing, tending
healing.

And in the whispering silence
could be heard the voice of the turtle dove
and the wind sighing in the trees
across the moors and down the rivers
to the sea.

'Love me, my love, love me
In the silence of your being, love me
in the silence of my being.'

In the beginning, God breathed...
and Some thing came into Being.

God is a verb.
God is not
a noun, a name, a thing.
God is a synonym
a metaphor
a flash of love between.
God is a way of being,
thinking, feeling
a relationship of love.

Iswaswillbe,
thennowtobe.
The YHWH of living.
The yaah-waay of breathing
metaphorically speaking
for that which cannot be spoken.

God is a pronoun,
he, she, it, I, thou, thee
transcending language
twisted by Man's forked tongue,
devised and divided,
the Absolute denied.

GOD IS NOT

God is not
a religious image hanging tidily,
dustily, on a cross safely out of reach.

God is life-breath.

God is not
kept in a holy cupboard
and brought out on Sunday
and other special occasions to worship
and people feel righteous and holy
and justified.

God is more insidious than that.
God sneaks into our breath and our being.
God slithers into our sinews and our bones.
God cleanses in our liver and our kidneys.
God composes rhythm and drumbeat
in our heart and in our blood.
God messes with our minds and our guts.

God is closer to you than you are to yourself.

Think on that – and tremble.

I have a thousand names
and none.
I am whispered down the wind
I am written in the flight of starlings
and croaked
in the earnest conversation of rooks.

I have a thousand names
and none.
I am spoken of between oak
and ash.
I laugh with the shivering leaves
of rowan and willow
and am fragranced in the blossom
of apple and hawthorn.

I have a thousand names
and none.
Hills and mountains bow and murmur
as I pass by.
Rivers and streams sigh
'It's you, it's you'
and with outstretched fingers
I touch their turmoil
into silken smoothness.

I have a thousand names
and none.

Who I am, I am.

Most of my life I have questioned words. What they mean, where they have come from, why they have been used in that order, why one word says more than another. Words are powerful, hurtful, calming, and can be manipulated and honed, altering the reader's/listener's perspective.

Poetry grants a freedom to construct meaning rather than instruct meaning. Language is not just a useful tool for conveying the mechanical instructions of knowledge and fact. The language of poetry breaks the dour habits of succinctness and logic, it cracks open the straight-jacket of received grammar and it allows thought to soar untethered into the stratosphere where imagination and intuition dance and sing. Poetry becomes a language we can trust to lead us to places not yet visited or dreamed of.

Like many of my era, poetry was an integral part of being taught English Literature – and it was always *English* Literature, even though it might be Scottish, Irish or Welsh. I came late to poetry from other cultures and countries. From my Catholic education I gleaned that Asian writings were unacceptable, American writing unheard of, and anything not Christian was sure to be pagan and ipso facto, avoided like the plague.

Studying the poetry of Shakespeare, Dante, Wordsworth and their ilk involved pulling the poem apart into their constituent grammatical components and being able to name them. As a mildly dyslexic person this made a nonsense of what I was reading – I literally lost the sense of the words. They made no sense. I lost interest in the classical writers. Such pedantry seemed to me somewhat akin to dissecting a frog, (we did that in Biology and rather revoltingly enjoyed it), pinning it to a board splayed out, labelled and enumerated, and then expecting it to jump when you poked it.

I found other poets to fill the vacuum. Roy Campbell, Rod McKuen, Joan Baez and Bob Dylan. Those were the early years…

Word, Spirit,
Spirit, Word, indivisible one and the same.
Ruach – Breath of God.

Word is not printed on a page
to be read by the literate few.

Word is to be breathed, sighed, whispered,
gossiped, spoken, shouted,
launched onto the wind.

Word will not be confined to buildings, books
or black-clad priests.

Word will be shared like a nourishing meal.
Word roams the streets, chilled by poverty
and despair.

Word breathes warmth into body, mind and
sick shattered soul.

Word breathes...
Spirit breathes...
...here I AM

Ruach – Breath of God

THE DNA OF GOD

the divine thread woven
into humankind woven
in the womb woven
from before time was

made in the image of God
imagined by God
to be not who we are
but who we may become

be divine

a child of God carrying the DNA
of God
fearfully, beautifully, lovingly
wonderfully made.

Of all the time and space
that ever was,
of all the random chaos of stars and moons
of ebb and flow of tides
and gravity –
in the spinning, unlikely cosmos came
a split-second of collision a single cell,
a pause between heartbeats, divided and doubled,
twisted and turned,
and helixed –
in a quiet echo
of the beginning of all that ever was.

'On the first day God spoke into the chaos...'

And so it began in all its terrible glory...
the never finished Story.

And in the fullness of time
came the lightning-strike,
the Godspark
made in the image of God...
us.

Shattered landscape...
Combestone Tor. October

Walking in the mist
groping to find a handhold
a foothold
on ewe-chewed, granite-strewn turf
I inch forward
as though playing some cosmic game
of blind-man's bluff.
There is nothing
no thing
to show where the next step must fall
only the falling away
of the ground and the pock-marked track where
cows and calves have been.

In the fog of the tentative footsteps
loom twisted, sharp hawthorn
bent, gnarled and eerie, lichened grey
like ancient inhabitants of a moor-swallowed
settlement
leaving behind only their sunken walls as
boundaries, way-mark gravestones.

Scarlet-robed rowan
shake their shocking fist-berries
in childish defiance
at the lowering cloud
cloud, shroud,
mothering, smothering.

No bird is heard,
no feathered flap betrays,
no clap of pigeon wings or
buzzard's mew.

And I, I inch painfully on lost
in a shattered landscape.

'...but the faith and the hope and the love are all in the waiting.'
T.S. ELIOT[2]

> Standing, straddling, stretching apart
> in the place of unknowing, something,
> some thing
> is waiting to be birthed.
> Pulled apart, weighed down, the pain
> distracts from what is being
> birthed.
> Standing in the place of unknowing
> the pain overwhelms the knowing
> of what is being born.

I do not want to spend the rest of my life hiding from myself. The fear is, that I am not brave enough to carry this through, although what 'this' is I cannot say. The fear is that the pain is so overwhelming that I may not be able to move beyond it and break through to whatever lies ahead. I am sure there is an ahead... the fear then, is not the pain. It is the letting go of the pain, familiar and known because it has been carried within since the original fear. Buried deeply, but liable to erupt like a long extinct volcano resurging.

    The fear is that in letting go, forgiveness will happen. And I am waiting for the forgiveness to be birthed. It has been a long gestation.

---

[2] East Coker

Why was the child so rebellious? Because she was judged by patriarchal Christianity and found to be wanting, that is why. Wanting because she was female and weak-willed, a sexual temptation. She needed to be guided in the error of her ways and disabused of her notions that God loved her as much as God loved boys. She was reliably told, aged fourteen, by a nun (the fount of all her religious knowledge), that she would never go to heaven. Heaven was reserved for Roman Catholics.

The patriarchal God, he of the Sistine Chapel, is overwhelming, overpowering, stifling. This God turns me into a 'non'. I am non-male, just as I once was non-Catholic. I become a non-person, non-existent, except through a male intermediary, in the eyes of this God.

'Who do you say that I am?'[3]

> I don't know who you are.
> I know who you are not.
>
> You are not the one sung to, feted
> and worshipped in the church.
> You are not that faded blond one
> who simpers from a wooden frame
> surrounded by bunny rabbits, bluebirds, flowers
> and children
> (one of whom is Black and naked
> while the others are in their national dress)
> You are not the one placidly dying, bleeding,
> on a cross.
>
> You might have been all those, once.
> But now?
>
> *'Who, now, do you say that I am?'*

---

[3] Matthew 16:15

Do not presume....

Do not pin the sacred
to a board and spread its pretty
wings so you may examine
it and exclaim
claim its beauty and your
ownership.

It will become a dead thing,
a lifeless thing, a relict
of faded, dusty glory
eternally pinned.

The sacred has no name, it is a feeling,
a stirring, a fluttering in the air,
in the innermost places that stretch and
call and beckon and
wheedle and cajole.

Do not presume...
The Sacred has no name.

Your God is too
small
You have limited
Your God
to his place
in Your universe.

Rather...

Look upon Your God
as the Totally-All
the Not-You.
The One who created you.
The Breather-of-the-Universe.

Rather...

Feel your God – mightily
and wonder.
Meet your God – somewhere
Other-than
yourself.

Can you make the grass grow?
Can you summon the wind?
Can you halt the tide
or stop the moon in her tracks?
Can you scent the cherry blossom
or hear a pine needle drop in the forest?

Thought not...

Have a little humility
Mortal...

I thank you God, whoever you are,
for the mithering mist and the enveloping silence
at the beginning of the day.

I thank you for the blessing of the first cup of coffee,
for the egg and mushrooms
and beans that go with them.

I delight, God in the fresh breeze making music
among the harebells
and the vapour trails criss-crossing the sky.

I rejoice in the barren rocks sheltering the
new born lamb
and I lift my eyes to the hills shining
with the night's dew.

Today God, I will face the day with borrowed
courage
and light hands and feet.
I will do what is necessary.

I will not be afraid of the coming hours
and what they may bring.
Today, God, I will delight in life and rejoice.

GREAT ELM.

'God so loved the world that he gave himself to it in his Son'

Actually –

God so loves the world that
God gives the Godself, continually
to it
in each and every one of us.
Laying the Loving open
to wounding and vulnerability,
to rejection and apathy.

And –

God continues,
eternally
to so love the world.

Love swallows up judgment.

God is
present
whether we are
or not.
God is...

You can fall out of love, but you can't fall out of God.

God is...

There is nothing
that God is
not.
God is
the above and below
God is
the beside and inside

God is
the space between words
the space between letters
hiding within
the full stops.

God is
the space between
breathing in
and out.

ABBEY HOUSE, GLASTONBURY.

One bedraggled
red rose,
bravely, soddenly
peering in through the window
me, sitting here –
inside, fed, dry.

What thinks it?
It's glory days long gone
with summer's heat.
Why is it
hanging on to its tattered
glimpses of glory?
What is its story,
what words is it using –
beating itself senseless against the window?

Drop by precious drop
its existence is eroded,
rotting, fading.
Tenaciously it clings
to its place in history.
Rooted deeply in the earth…

The day after…
the just about red rose,
two forlorn petals clinging on
stands proudly erect,
warming in the early morning sunshine.

Doesn't it know it has to let go of everything
before it can blossom again?

SECOND DAY – BUCKFAST ABBEY

Something is happening
in the silence...

Something like the slow leak
of air from a tyre,
of water from a tap's faulty washer.

Something like seawater through sand
breath from a punctured ball
slow releasing.
Something is happening, a deflation,
a dribbling away of all that is vital.

Something is happening
and it doesn't seem as if it can be stopped
at all.
Quietly, wearily precious lifeblood
is trickling into the sand
between the cracks in the pavement
and down the drains
leaving only tiredness,
deflation, flatness
breathlessness...

In the desert angels minister.

This is my garden.
It may be full of weeds,
nettles and dandelions and bindweed,
but it is my garden.

It has pools where dragonflies
hover and dance,
it has roses who fall over and cling
to each other.

It has snail-trails and slug-slime,
it has water lilies and frog spawn,
healing herbs and honeysuckle and
ripe raspberries.

Ants cultivate, wasps salivate,
birds thieve and it is unique,
it is universal, it is my cosmos
and my sacred place,
my garden, the ground of my being

is this satisfying or
do you want to go in deeper?
to take your feet off the bottom
and trust that you can swim?

or at least keep your head above water.

"What if..." says the monkey-mind
what if you don't swim
or at least keep your head above water?

what if you sink
what if lungs fill
not with life-breathing air
but death-dealing water –
what then?

Do you trust
that in the chaos
of drowning
of gasping for air
of flailing arms

I was not waving but drowning..." [4]

there will come a dying
a stillness
a peace
and a rebirth...

and you will learn how to swim.

---

[4] *Not Waving but Drowning.* Stevie Smith. 1957

On the road less travelled
am I coming or going?
Where am I going
or where am I coming from –
are my boundaries
broken
or am I well-fenced in?
that will make all the difference.

over the barbed-wire fence heedless
of ripped flesh
crossing the boundaries
to climb the hill, to fly the kite
in soaring imagination sailing
where it will
tugging and dipping, yearning for freedom
to skim the earth, to skim the clouds
living life dangerously trusting
that the string will not be let go...

Just get over the barbed wire
fence and
fly
that will make all the difference.

My life is a half-finished
sentence
a world of
unfinished phrases and
unsaid words.

My prayer is a jumble
of thoughts a
tangle of brightly coloured
wool an unfinished garment.

My silence is full of noise and
non sense.
Where is this place
I have been put,
have put myself?

Where will it lead –
to the desert –
to the wilderness –
where angels minister?

To thirst-quenching springs and crocus blossoming?
This is my Way
my Truth, my Life
and
it is not at all comfortable

My soul is between stories.
What has gone before
no longer fits,
the story is not true,
it is a bed-time story,
comforting, sleep-inducing, saccharine,
a "and they all lived happily ever after"
kind of story.

The new story is not yet written, quite.
But it is spoken,
told around campfires,
it is whispered over coffee cups,
carried on the breeze,
given to girl childs
on their birth day.

The story will be theirs to tell
in their voice,
of relationships, singing of weaving their lives
into rich tapestries of birth and death
and re-creation,
of nurture and nature inter woven
with bright colour, subtle shades and
dark storms – earth pulled, moon-pulled,
tide-told,
a fabric so strong that it carries
the new story across oceans and
continents
and never, ever, spills
a single precious drop.

This time, the story won't be lost,
mislaid, silenced.

IGNATIAN JOURNEY, BUCKFAST.

reach back to touch
the child you were –
beyond your outstretched fingertips
she is there
sitting on the step
in the sunlight
before the Fall
playing with spiders and woodlice
knowing she is safe
and loved
she is there looking in awe
in the ivy on the old stone wall
for snails and birds' nests and slowworms
in the blackcurrant bushes,
at the bottom of the garden by the old greenhouse,
in the tadpole-soaked pond crawling with
water boatmen
and damselflies.

she is still there – walled up
to keep her safe from harmful things that creep,
in the night
reach back –
and with outstretched,
bleeding fingers dismantle
the stones brick by painful brick
and pull her out of the tomb you made
to keep her safe
set her free so she can fly
and you.

ABBEY HOUSE, NOVEMBER.

The black bats of fear
swirl and swoop
around the corridors of my mind
poking and prying
with radar-sharp precision.

Sick to my stomach I call
for the help I cannot find.
Dread thoughts, negative spheres
wolves and lions
dance their macabre waltz
and I am lost in their deathly rhythms.

Where are the bright lights of love?
What more must I do
what less must I do?
Am I ripped apart or
re-membered...?

There is a cavernous space
inside
where I used to be
abhorring a vacuum,
nature is uneasy
but waits uneasily with me
for what comes next

if there is nothing next
who will I be?

THE ROAD TO ORLIGIANO, OCTOBER.

It occurs to me that I am frightened to move into another day. Yesterday I stepped into the day and felt nothing. I saw plenty. Mountain roads writhing back on themselves, like snakes. Pretty stone houses, roman-tiled, with roses clambering over them. Pine and oak, hawthorn's red berries, food for wintering birds. Ancient hilltop towns and villages piled slap-dash onto the hill's sides. Flowers and crops, cathedrals and cats. I saw it all – and felt nothing.

   I am frightened to step into today and see everything and feel nothing. I have lost not only the joy but the will to even feel the joy. My throat closes against despair, but it leaks from my eyes, anyway.

Something is over – something has ended.
The grief would come and the healing begin
if the something were known,
understood, comprehended.

But the something is unreachable,
unnameable, unknowable.
What now?
No grief, no tears, no healing,
just an indefinable, unpindownable
pain, a numbing ache
that sends the soul scurrying
back into its crevasse, down
to Persephone's winter.

Not one seed of the pomegranate
is split.
or spilt.

HOMESICK

What is the point of being a voice crying
in the wilderness?
Who is there who hears?
Who is there who cares?

Small lizards scurry to hide.
Vultures glide above on unseen thermals.
Ibex bound from crag to rock face,
death defiant...

and the mountain lion, belly empty sniffs the
scent laden air.

No-one, no thing hears
the voice crying in the wilderness.
No-one, no thing knows the pain, despair,
wounded fear.

All there is, is there weeping, wilderness, emptiness.
Who knows, who cares,
when a tree falls in the forest?
Who hears, if no-one is there?

When you are in the dark
drowning
thrashing about in the depths
of your sea of despair

when there is no raft
to clamber on no lifebelt to cling to

that is when you learn to trust
your body and the Godself
inside...
...and you float.

There is no pleasant way of drowning
you just let go and wait

WILD GOOSE CHASE

> Never cease seeking…
> There is no ending,
> only yet another beginning.
>
> The tired soul –
> yearning to rest is yet
> prodded on.
>
> There is no finality, only
> a continuing journey,
> whose way is not known
> whose horizon is not seen
> whose meaning is not grasped.

Peace of mind nor happiness cannot be bought by money or made by machine. It cannot be gained by success or a high standard of living. The truth is it must be worked for, effort must be made and energy expended, mined from the depth of one's being. It is where the real revelations dwell. And for those one must sit still and do nothing but perhaps, listen. And that is hard…

> Keep things small –
> on a human scale
> able to be held, treasured
> in a human hand –
> the rest is
> Babel.

> Alone, today
> in pain for them,
> for me.
>
> Dreams shattered,
> hope turned to ashes.
> Alone.
>
> There is nothing left to mend.
> There is no future, just past
> might-have-beens.
>
> Alone.
> Again. Each of us.
> Isolated in our separate pain.

"...we can see how the more we lose our sense of separateness in the knowledge of the oneness of all living creatures, millions of small leaves on the one single tree of life..."

ELIZABETH GOUGE. THE JOY OF SNOW. P71

Organised religion has become a problem for me. It began with "Our Father…" and my Catholic convent education. If God is male, then male is god. It began with the priest walking into class and interrupting lessons to fire catechism questions. *"Who made you?" "God made me"* we would all chant back. *"Why did God make you?" "God made me to know, love and obey Him.",* we obediently replied. It was of course an all-girls school. We never questioned why the only man permitted on the premises – apart from Alec the gardener – was able to interrupt Geography, English, Maths or Science, we just did as we were told, after all, that was what the Blessed Virgin Mary did. *"It shall be as you say."*

Nuns told me I was a dirty little girl. They told me that God loved me but that as I wasn't a Catholic, I wouldn't go to heaven. Drop by poisonous drop I learned that love was to be avoided.

We all knew that as the weaker, easily led sex we had a choice – we could be Eve, or we could be Mary. Being Eve was a very bad thing to be. Being Mary was impossible. Eve was responsible for all the woes of the world. It was she who picked the fruit from the Tree of Knowledge of Good and Evil. No one pointed out what a weak-kneed individual Adam was for going along with it. *"The woman made me do it"* he whined…

There are only a few mentions of Jesus worshipping on the Sabbath. Mostly when he wanted to be with his God, his Parent, he withdrew from the world and from people, he took time apart. *"Pray in your room"* he said. Jesus could be found on the roads, in people's houses, on the hills and by the lakeside. Why should it be any different now? He will be in the hospitals, in the parks, in the homes of the lonely and abused. He will be at the football match and in the supermarket. He will be wherever people are. He's probably in church too. I go there occasionally, just to check. I do catch glimpses of him from time to time.

It is very nice to meet on Sundays and worship together; it makes us feel good and it makes us feel loved and we need that. It gives us strength and hope. But do not mistake Sunday worship for being Christian. That is not what being a follower of Jesus is about. Go into your room and meet with your God and then go out on your journey – and meet God's people, all of them, whoever and whatever they might be.

> "It's all very well and nice to worship Jesus – but following Jesus – ah! That would make all the difference."
>
> RICHARD ROHR. FRANCISCAN PRIEST AND WRITER.

Ask yourself
woman
ask yourself.
"Is it man-made?"

This thought, this cherished belief
this way of being,
where did it come from?

What is your inheritance
woman?
Who are your ancestors?
In whose womb were you woven?
Were you man-made
woman?

Your breath is yours alone
breathe it,
form your words from it,
weave your own history,
faith-story, tradition,
re-claim your ancestors,
grandmothers,
re-claim yourself
woman.

Not man-made,
woman-woven.

It would be a start
to know what the start is,
but then what?

Shall I sit and wait
for a meaningful way to worship,
a meaningful moment to cling to?

Do I hang around, marking time,
needing support until I stumble
into other women doing the same?

I have lost my lode-star
I have displaced, misplaced
my magnetic North.

I'm spinning, endlessly in confusion
giddy with dizziness, no up, no down,
a sycamore key, helecoptering,
earth-bound,
feeling the pull of gravity,
helpless to resist the Laws.

If I lose gravity
might I teach myself to fly?

"Do you know what
 God?"...
"No, neither do I."

Mary Magdalene, according to legend, brought the Holy Grail, the 'Sangraal' across the Mediterranean Sea to France, to Saintes Marie. What the Holy Grail was is not known. Speculation has it that it is the cup Jesus used at the last meal. Or it might be the cup that caught Jesus' precious blood at the crucifixion. Later stories assert that the Sangraal is not an object but a bloodline tracing back to Jesus and Mary Magdalene. (I was taught, in the 1950's, that Mary Magdalene was a prostitute. Even though I didn't know what such a thing was, it was obviously not a good thing to be).

What if the dark Sarah, the one, who accompanied Mary Magdalene, Mary Salome and Mary Jacobi (or Clopas) and landed in Saintes-Maries-de-la-Mer in around 42ce was not an Egyptian servant who accompanied the Marys, but the child of Mary Magdalene – the girl child born 'out of Egypt'. The flight into Egypt might then have been a race-memory, not of the Holy Family of Mary, Joseph and the infant Jesus, but perhaps of that other Mary and Joseph – Magdalen and Arimathea, to protect Jesus' unborn child. Heresy of course...

The Gospel of Philip says: *'There were three who walked with the Lord at all times; Mary, his mother, her sister, and Magdalene, the one who is called his companion...'* Of course, such a notion is non-canonical and therefore probably heretical too...

This idea has proved too radical for a patriarchal church. It was only much, much later that I discovered that the notion of heresy does not necessarily rest on truth, but whether or not the statement is in line with the official statement of faith. Good churchmen revere the chalice and weave it into their worship in remembrance of a radical rabble-rouser. Arthurians wove stories of distressed maidens, chivalry, and troubadours, and goodness only knows what the Knights Templar were about... so the search continues. And given the number of true relics of the cross, of bits of saints hoarded in churches and scattered across the centuries, it seems to be to be just a bit convenient that this holiest of all holy objects was somehow misplaced, lost in the mists of time, buried at Avalon or somewhere in Scotland, or who knows where.

These are men's stories. But what of the women's stories. What if women have always known what the Holy Grail is and where it is? What if that knowledge has been driven so deep underground by centuries of male religion that woman have forgotten how to connect themselves to their own wisdom?

'The king is wounded and crippled and the kingdom has become a wasteland because the Grail is lost. The story promises that when the sacred vessel that once contained the blood of Christ is found, the king will be healed and all will be well.'[5]

What if you substitute 'queen' for 'king'?

---

[5] The Woman with the Alabaster Jar. Margaret Starbird p23.

The Gentile woman stood her ground,
Persisted, argued, fought for her children.
'Even the dogs get the crumbs from the table.'
she yelled in his face.

Is this what you call love?

Me, I can't even gather
the crumbs.
The face of God is implacably turned away
and Jesus has left the room.

Another woman
judged and found wanting.

You can't have it all ways
God.
Although, being God,
perhaps you think you can.

I am an old woman now – disregarded by age and gender. I am past childbearing, just as Sarah and Elizabeth were. What is now expected of me? Shall I laugh as Sarah did? Shall I rejoice as Elizabeth did? This gestation is a long time coming...

Let me teach you, God
about what it is like
to be human – me.

When hopes are raised
then dashed.
The first time, it is disappointing
but bearable.

The second time the dream is realised
then snatched away
it is upsetting but you pull yourself together...
...are you with me so far, God?

The third, fourth, fifth times
you think "this must be it now, it feels right"
and yet still the vision, it eludes
and you awaken to the usual desolation,
disillusion.

"Hope" you say.
"Trust" you say.

But what you don't know, God
being God and all
is that being human and all
you run out of hope and trust
and God...

Because I'm only human.

A very devout Christian named Grace died and very nervously stood waiting for God's judgement. As she waited she became more and more anxious thinking about her life and how little she had achieved. She imagined God asking her *"Why weren't you Sarah, or Mother Teresa, Esther or Rosa Parks?".*
 Just then God appeared and asked, *"Why weren't you Grace?"*

DREAM...

I saw a wounded bird – a gull I thought at first – waiting on a low red brick wall behind which a shrub with yellow berries was growing. Every now and then the bird became restless and struggled to its feet, its eyes fixed on a dark red door opposite.

   I looked away for a moment into a shop window next to the red door. When I looked back a young woman was sitting on the low brick wall with the bird in her lap. The bird didn't struggle but offered its hurt head and the wound under its wing to the young woman. She pulled out the thorns she found there.

   Then I thought – this is not a gull, this is a dove, and the young woman is God and I am the bird. And then I thought – perhaps the bird is God and I am the young woman.

'God is good. The world is good. You are good.'
RICHARD ROHR. 'THE WISDOM PATTERN' 2020

Do you think a dream
is nothing at all?
You are made of the stuff
of dreams.
God dreamt you
and saw that you were good
and every good thing
comes from God.

God made in you
the thing that dreams
the imagination that pushes you
beyond your self.
God made in you
that which enables you to dream
the wildest dreams
and when you have learned to trust

God knows what is good for you.
Then your wildest dreams
will become
reality.

KENTUCKY, SEPTEMBER.

We have forgotten how to think for ourselves. Our minds, our bodies and our imagination have grown fat and lazy. We are no longer in control of our food, our water, our heat and light, our shelter. Even the air is not free anymore. We meekly accept what is offered and pay through the nose for it.

How does this Multiconglomerate economy benefit us? It doesn't. it benefits the shareholders. It benefits huge global, faceless multinationals. We are merely purchasers of commodities. We buy things we could well obtain for ourselves for a small outlay and physical work. And let me say here – work is not a dirty word. Work is what keeps us healthy, whole and sane.

Given a small piece of land – a garden, a patch of earth, a pot, each of us can grow *something*. A flower, an apple tree, a row of lettuce, tomatoes. And the first time we do and we look at the beauty of what, with our hands and sweat, and air and water, we have grown, we enter into a covenant – a covenant with Creation, God, Nature, call it what you will – a covenant with Something Other Than. This covenant cannot be bought, cannot be owned and there are no bank accounts to be held up. This covenant just is. It exists between us and the little bit of land and the plant we have grown. A Trinity passed on of lore, wisdom and love from parent to child.

The year I was born the world changed, the year after the Second World War. How do I know that more than seventy seven years on? Because farming has changed. How the land was thought of, about, changed. Land had been the provider, for family and for the wider community. Land was walked, nurtured, seeded, tilled, cropped. Land was intimately known. Land was worked with, not fought against.

Hope and Innovation, those two feral children charged into the world. Hope whispered false promises. "This can be done better, faster, cheaper, giving you more time to do the things you *really* want to do." Innovation shouted "Buy this washing machine, tractor, power tool, dish washer. You will do things faster (but not necessarily better). You won't be a slave to work, to drudgery anymore."

Now land is another commodity and the animals kept on the land – if indeed they are allowed on to it – are units in a factory called agribusiness. Where is the sense in housing 400 cows all the year around and having to haul their food to them and haul their dung away from them? Go near any industrial farm unit and you will meet feed lorries trucking in feed at all hours of the day and night. Country lanes have become an endless motorway of tractors and slurry tankers, like monstrous ants in their search for somewhere to spread their cargo. What is this doing to the environment, this endless parade of vehicles? And do not get me started on the health and lifespan of these poor beasts that provide our daily pint.

In the year I was born there was a beast called the dual-purpose cow. She may have been a Dairy Shorthorn. She could provide milk and meat. It all worked on a rather small scale. But it did work. That was before we were encouraged to drink more milk and eat more meat. That was before the McDonaldisation of food.

And the land became a commodity too. Family farms which supported a family and the local community have given way to vacuum cleaner designers and sugar barons who buy up land and employ strangers to run their robotic agri-businesses while their profits are stacked away in offshore banks and legitimate tax evasion. So bedazzled were we by these infants' charm and beauty that we fell out of love with work that kept our minds and bodies and spirits healthy and fit and earned us deep rest at evening's close. Life could indeed be harsh and unyielding and poverty-stricken, and people died of disease and hunger and lack of care, the year I was born.

So, we sought to relieve the poverty, the hunger, the disease by Acts of Parliament, Education Acts, the National Health Service, the Ministry of Agriculture, Food and Fisheries. Hope and Innovation grew to be rambunctious teenagers and swept along by their infectious enthusiasm we joined in their rock and roll. We called for 'traditional values' and they answered, 'New Look', 'Units of Production', 'Progress' without ever saying progress towards what, and for what end.

We no longer worked for or with or within our community or our neighbourhood. We travel to work and from work. Work is a place we go. Work is not what we do with our lives mostly. The Terrible Twins replaced independence, skill, intelligence, pride, loyalty, innovation and respect with productive units, man-hours (not women-hours, you will note, man-hours are the only ones of *real* value), and human resources. People ceased to be 'personnel' and became 'resources.

And women most of all, fell for their lies. "You can have it all.", they said. And so it was. You can go to work to pay for your house, your washing machine, your leisure *and* you get to raise the children clean the house, bake the cakes, and do the washing as well. Now, isn't that progress?

Progress – that deceitful word
a word that sounds good
something to strive for
work towards
a goal to aim for.

Progress – that lying word
promising something better,
more time, more money
more – of what
you already had.

Progress – a flimsy tissue
elusive, blown by the wind
always dancing enticingly ahead
like a gaudy butterfly
calling 'chase me, capture me
and you will possess me!'

Lies and illusion, all.

'To have everything but money is to have much.'
WENDELL BERRY. 'THE WORLD-ENDING FIRE' P108

Peace of mind, nor happiness, cannot be bought by money or made by machine. It cannot be gained by success or extravagant living. It must be worked for, effort must be made, energy expended. It must be mined from the depths of one's being. It is where real revelations dwell.

We had it all
and we gave it away –
exchanged it for a mess of pottage.

We gave away
our right to grow our own good food
for an illusion –
skinny fries and a burger.

We gave away
our self-sufficiency,
light, air, water – free gifts
for a costly share of oil, gas, electricity,
fossils in exchange
for life-giving sustainability.

Worst of all,
we gave away our ancestral stories.
"Remember when Granfer harnessed the bay cob
and it ran off with the cart?"
"Remember that autumn with the bumper crop
of quince
and we had Quince Jelly all winter long?"

Remember?
We have forgotten our family stories,
our place in the history of our land.
We have no land.

We have no need of stories –
we have Soaps and Celebrity and Strictly.
We live vicariously,
through overwrought imitations of Life.

We had it all – except money.
And just look
at what money has given us.
We have lost it all.

THOUGHTS ON THE HOMESTEAD - KENTUCKY

It was the door latch that got to me. At first glance a simple, primitive thing. Set into the stout, rough-hewn door is a piece of bent metal and an iron pin. No nails, just a hole that the hand forged chain went through, a groove rubbed smooth by years of use, the weighted end keeping the flies and critturs out.

Doubled back on itself the iron bow fixed neatly over the pin in the plank of the wall and held the door fast. Planks from the sawmill down by the stream, iron fashioned in the blacksmiths shop, homespun, homemade, homestead.

And the fools think it is the farmers who are stupid.

> We do not own the land
> it does not belong to us.
> We have custody of it
> as we have custody of our children.
>
> We have no rights to the land.
> We have a loving duty of care for it,
> to want what keeps it healthy and fertile
> and beautiful,
> as we would for our children.
>
> We do not own the land,
> we must not diminish,
> pollute, disfigure or poison it
> as we would not our children.
>
> When it comes right down to it
> we owe our lives, our health,
> our souls to the land.
> When we destroy it, we destroy ourselves –
> and our children.

In that time spent visiting family in Kentucky I was invited to the home of Wendell and Tina Berry. Wendell Berry is a poet, an agronomist, a writer and I guess most of all, a farmer. His poetry is the poetry of place and belonging, his writing full of wisdom and lore. We spent a few hours in his kitchen talking of politics and farming, rural life and country people. He told me how he had lost hope in America and agriculture, in big agribusiness that no longer serves the community in which it is planted. I was shocked by the loss of hope from this gentle Christian man. And then he went on to say, "...so I just do what I can where I am." I carry these wise and profound words with me. They tell me that Berry has not lost hope. He just does what he can where he is. And that is all any of us can do...

REAL LIFE

> Margins and edges
> where ploughed field meets hedge,
> where tumbling sea meets shore
> where domed sky meets the horizon.
>
> Margins and edges
> where the withy drinks from streams
> where deer shade from midday sun
> where prey shelters from predator.
>
> In long grass,
> stone walls,
> ditches and rock pools
> where wilderness comes to meet us
> and upsets our domestic tidy minds
> of how things ought to be.

We are limited, defined, boundaried. The very definition 'human being' limits us. We are what we are. We are not flying creatures, burrowing creatures or swimming creatures though we can do all those things in a limited sort of way. We are evolved bi-peds. Walking creatures, feet on the earth – limited by our stride. Only God is limitless. And we have not understood that. We think we are God.

Women were the first farmers – it's obvious really. Who were the plant gatherers who couldn't stray far from home because of child-bearing and child-rearing? Gathering seeds and berries and nuts and seeing seedlings and saplings growing, the thought must have arisen that rather than wander haphazardly from place to place looking for food, why not gather the seeds and plant them in one place where they could be nurtured and tended? Likewise, perhaps much later, wouldn't it be easier to domesticate animals and raise their young for food and milk for their young and themselves?

Let the men go out on their hunts risking life and limb. Hunting as a way of food-gathering had huge rewards in terms of usage but also too, a huge toll. Much safer to raise and grow your own near to water and your settlement. And in doing so, raising the odds of your children's survival.

So when did women become the weaker sex......?

> Girls don't climb trees
> it's not lady-like.
> Boys climb trees.
> It's what boys do.
>
> Girls don't climb trees
> they might show their knickers.
> Boys climb trees.
> It's tough and manly
> and they wear jeans.
>
> Girls don't wear jeans
> dresses and skirts are prettier and daintier
> and you mustn't get them dirty
> climbing trees.
> Boys wear jeans
> and get them dirty
> because Dad wears jeans
> and if they get dirty,
> Mummy washes them
> because Dad is the boss.
>
> Girls can't be the boss.
> It's not nice, or feminine
> and it says so in the Bible.
> Boys can be the boss.
> They are born to be
> because they are boys.
>
> Girls! Wear jeans
> and climb trees!

Feminist is a word that needs qualifying and I am not qualified to do that. I am old enough to remember the feminists of the 1960's and early 1970's. The burn your bra brigade and make love not war hippy movement, the poke a flower down the barrel of a gun lot. Germaine Greer arrived on the scene but I was distracted by the death of my mother when she was 52 and I was 28, pregnant with my first child. I remained distracted for the next 16 years. I was intimidated by my doctor who told me I was making a fuss when I miscarried my second child. I was outraged when the hospital needed my husband's permission when I wanted no more children after my third child was born and asked to be sterilized. I stopped going to church when I was asked to take my fidgeting child out as it was distracting the local pillar of the community from worshipping.

I now discover that there are many kinds of feminist and I do not belong with any of them. I don't hate men, I am not Black, nor Asian, nor LGBTQ+. I probably don't count as a feminist anyway being a white, middle-class and elderly, woman. But in my head, and in my heart and soul I am a feminist.

Feminism, my brand, has brought my faith into vivid focus. What was once dull and repetitive ritual has gained meaning and life. There is a downside to this. I have harsh things to say about the injustice of female inequality and church and society's patriarchy, and people are challenged and threatened by that. I have often been like the prophet Amos and told "Go back to the North and tend your fig trees".

Feminism, my brand, led me to keeping my surname when I remarried after divorce. I chose to use my mother's maiden name as I wanted nothing to do with the one on my birth certificate. And yet I still, after more than 27 years of marriage, get addressed by my husband's surname. And to compound my membership of the awkward squad I claim my right to my title – Reverend. It is not gender specific and that suits me. Who needs to know whether I am female or male other than perhaps my doctor? I don't use Mrs, Ms or Miss, I use Rev'd. And that was fine apart from the odd occasions at public things where my husband was warmly shaken by the hand and greeted "Ah! You must be Reverend Steele!" because of course we all know that vicars (and I am a minister) are male. As are doctors, and farmers, and scientists and engineers...

I used to see myself as a child and God as my Father – because that is what I was taught. And a father can be abusive, so did that make God abusive too? What I have learned is that I am an adult in whom God lives. I think of God as truth, life, energy and most of all, Love. One-sided naming of God runs the real risk of idolatry and it distorts our relationship with God.

From the time we are young we are taught that what is most sacred is male. Women have never had their full identity affirmed as men do, being made in the image of God. It is difficult then, for women to believe wholly in their own sacredness, their own autonomy, their own capacity to imagine God.

Think about it: God as Father, King, Lord – goes without saying – male.

Now think about: God as Mother, Gentle Wind, Wisdom, Woman in Childbirth – female.

Where have you ever seen or read the feminine side of God? And yet, we are told, we are all made in the image of God. What does that tell you about God?

Insultingly I have now been robbed of my professional title. Has this happened to doctors and aristocrats? No. However if you have your car insurance through LV or try to order something from Marks and Spencer on-line you must choose to be Mrs, Miss, Ms and bizarrely Mx, because there isn't a box to tick for Reverend. And you must tick the boxes because the computer program will not let you move on until you do. Why isn't my name enough? I no longer shop online with many companies including Marks and Spencer because they don't have a box to tick for Reverend. LV insisted on Ms – whatever that means. Sometimes I get mail addressed to Dr. And once, wonderfully, I was addressed as 'Other Angela Steele'. Brilliant!

What renews me and fills me with hope, for women, and men who support women, is that Mary Magdalene was the first person to receive a resurrection appearance. And it was she who was called to be the apostle to the apostles. The way that women have been and are treated does not in any way reflect the mind of Jesus. Despite all the rumours, fantasies and besmirching of her, Mary Magdalen stands as a beacon for women.

Jesus' maleness has been used against women despite all the evidence to the contrary – and it is not my purpose to enumerate them – look for yourself. Women have been and still are, excluded from their rightful place in the Church. And society apes the Church. Not so much now that the Church has less influence but foundationally all our laws, traditions and culture are based on the patriarchy of the Church. It is little wonder that many women reject organised religion and struggle to find a right relationship with their God – or simply give up.

Any relationship I might have with Jesus – and it is still tenuous – is due to those writers who sought and seek to give Mary Magdalene her rightful place. And I am not talking Dan Browne here. Thanks to my 1950's Catholic convent education I was taught that she was a prostitute and that was a bad thing to be. I knew that I was a protestant and wasn't going to go to heaven – one of the nuns who taught us RI had told me so, only Catholics were allowed in. So, was I a very bad thing? I left the convent aged sixteen very muddled and with two O Levels to my name – English Literature and Religious Instruction. I have digressed.

The historical once-and-for-all Jesus must not be mistaken for the universal Christ. Christ-in-the-world takes many forms and guises. He can be seen in the Big Issue Seller, the single mother struggling to bring up her children, the trafficked sex slave and the migrant worker. Christ can be seen in the Muslim social worker, the Black midwife, the Jewish peacemaker, and the Asian factory worker. The resurrection body of Jesus the Christ transcends male and female limitations. The risen Christ is the One Body and, as we are taught, we are all an integral part of the One Body. The powerful image of Christ in bread and wine says it all. Grown in the earth by the mystery of the soil and the water and the wind (or God), tended and loved by human hands, shaped and nurtured by the elements it requires a whole universe in order to offer back to God bread and wine.

Jesus' naming of himself as Vine, Water, Bread and Mother Hen connects him to the earth and its sacredness. Julian of Norwich says of Jesus;

"And our saviour is our true Mother, in whom we are endlessly born and out of whom we shall never come." p292[6]

---

[6] Showings. Trans. Edmund College & James Walsh. 1985

> "Do small things with great love."
> MOTHER TERESA

become world-rattling,

when doing the small things
of life
become world-rattling
do not do small things
in a mimsy, pimsy,
mean way, a pursed mouthed
kind of way
do the small things large –
rattle the world
do the large things loudly
don't whisper them
yell them
upset the apple cart
tip over the shopping trolley
ruffle the feathers
overturn the tables,
let the pigeons come home to roost –
become world-rattling.

The experience of women mystics demonstrates that it is possible to relate to Jesus in a way that does not glorify male reality at the expense of female experience. Where are the modern women mystics? Where is the incarnation of God in terms of female experience? The institutional church has many subtle ways of denying and betraying Jesus' message regarding women. Historically it was important that Jesus was male. Only a male at that time and in that context could critique and challenge tradition and the Law. Women identify with Jesus because there is a shared vision that is not based on gender and status. Resurrection happens in reconciliation.

> I love the men
> who have those fine
> feminine qualities of empathy
> and vulnerability,
> who can be moved to tears
> by devastation and beauty.
>
> I love the men who
> have those unsuspected
> female strengths of staying power
> and grit
> who can heal and reconcile
> the broken-hearted and downtrodden.
>
> I pity the men
> who cannot walk the mile
> in women's shoes.
> They only know the half
> of the cross
> and resurrection.
> I love them too...
> occasionally.

Violence and abuse against women have been taken for granted for so long. "She asked for it dressed like that." "She deserved it." "Look at the way she behaves...". Women are accustomed to bearing the blame. If they got pregnant in the not so far away past, it was their fault, as if they did it all by themselves. The spectre of Eve raised her seductive head. It was never a man's fault. It was always the woman who was the temptress. *"The woman made me do it."* bleated Adam and set a precedent for every male thereafter.

Generations of women have turned to the Bible for inspiration and comfort, relying on the Word to give them courage and grace. As they read and digest and meditate many become aware that this is a scripture written by men for men and has been used to dominate and justify women's subservient role. How can women relate to, and trust, writings that are the outcome of a patriarchal culture? How can the Bible be the Word of God for women when women's lives have largely been written out of it?

There are few women's stories that are related by more than just a passing mention of a name. There is Sarah, whom when danger threatened, Abram tried to pass off as his sister and then was betrayed by him with her servant Hagar in order that he should have an heir. We are told Sarah laughed when she was told she would have a child in her old age as if that were some kind of sin. I would not have laughed; I would have cried – imagine giving birth at her age. Hagar, at Sarah's insistence – she was only human after all – was thrown out with her son into the desert to die. She was just a servant, a sex slave and probably black, so Abraham abandoned her and his son. But God didn't.

And then we have Mary, the Mother of God, Theatokus, (Yes, I do know how to spell!) God-Bearer, mother of Jesus who was turned into a perpetual virginal mother. We know Jesus had brothers and probably sisters too so why does the Church persist in its depiction of this strong, virile, brave woman as a meek milk-and-water virginal child? Isn't that just a bit creepy?

Why isn't more attention paid to the stories of the women in Exodus? There are the midwives, Puah and Shiphrah who concealed the birth of little boys, there is Moses' mother, and her daughter, who saved Moses and there is the pharaoh's daughter who took him in and raised him. And of course, there's Eve who is to blame for everything.

Now do you notice that it is the women who begin the liberation of the people by refusing to submit to oppression? Read carefully, with wisdom and insight and compassion, the Bible makes sense of our experiences and gives meaning to our lives. Despite, or maybe because of, the Bible's patriarchal context and inconsistencies, despite its mixed messages, its silences and its outrageous shoutings, read with an open mind and with love; scripture is above all the story of God's love affair with all of creation, no matter how much man tries to prove differently. It leads us all, if we are listening and if we are paying attention, to a God who is creating and ever recreating. *'For lo! I saw a New Heaven and a New Earth...'[7]*, clearly one that challenges existing cultural, social and religious practices and speaks on behalf of the poor, the outcast and the oppressed. Women want more than 'crumbs from under the table'. The demand is to sit at the table along with the rest of disenfranchised humanity. The demand is that the 'Men Only' sign be trampled underfoot.

Refusal to listen by those who exercise patriarchal/hierarchical power is, paradoxically, a fatal weakness stemming from a fear of loss of power and status that is ultimately disempowering men and their religion. Women know how to empower others. They do it by giving their power away. They give it to their children and those they nurture and care for. It is sad that so few men have learned this. Women do it through their art, their craft, their music, their dance and they do it through their relationships.

> Where were the women?
> Where were the women
> when Mary laboured
> to push Jesus out into an uncaring world?
>
> Where were the women
> when Jesus walked the dusty roads
> telling his stories of nonsense and hope?
> Who did his washing?
>
> Where were the women
> who prepared the last supper
> while the men sat down to celebrate
> and grieve the Passover? Who did the washing up?
>
> Where were the women
> on that long walk on the Via Dolorosa, at Golgotha
> when that broken body was taken down
> and entombed?
> Who comforted the sorrowing?
>
> Where were the women
> on the road to Emmaus,
> in the house where tongues of fire were seen?
> Where are all the women?

---

[7] Revelation 21:1

GREAT ELM. JULY.

'God so loved the world that he gave himself to it in his son.'[8]

Actually –

God so loves the world that
God gives the Godself, continually
to it
in each and every one of us.
Laying the Loving open to
rejection and apathy.

And –

God continues eternally
to so love the world.

Love swallows up judgment.

---

[8] John 3:16

the only way to deal with horror,
when small and helpless,
is to shut it down and let numbness
be a comforting cave in which to crawl.

even now, a lifetime away,
there is a place within, walled-up,
impregnable, a safe citadel where you,
God, cannot penetrate.

this is what you, Abuser,
did to me.
rendered my self, my soul,
God without.

but you, Abuser, do not triumph
over my body as before you did,
over the body of a small defenceless girl-child.
how brave and strong were you then.

God will find a way in and she will comfort me...

It is time to uncover
and discover
what is true.

It is time to discover
what is chaff, husk
necessary for its time
to protect and nurture
but now,

time for the carapace to be blown away
on the wind
dropped

once more into the dark earth and
allow the vulnerable,
fragile soul-self
to blossom.

It is time to uncover a heart that sings.

The Cosmic Christ is not the Jesus of the first century although that is where the awareness is awakened and brought to life. The Cosmic Christ lives and breathes and has their being wherever there is oppression, injustice, war and famine and someone shouts *"No! not in my God's name."*

Stop trying to read the mind of God. It is a strategy for avoiding what we do not want to do. We ask ourselves "Does God really want me to do this?" and then decide to wait and see. That is how nothing gets done. It is said: "The only thing necessary for the triumph of evil is for good people to do nothing."[9] Do it anyway. If it is not God-sent, whatever it is will not work and you will be rescued.

A far wiser person than me once wrote:

> My Lord God
> I have no idea where I am going.
> I do not see the road ahead of me.
> I cannot know for certain where it will end.
> Nor do I really know myself,
> and the fact that I think I am following your will
> does not mean that I am actually doing so.
> But I believe that the desire to please you
> does in fact please you.
> And I hope I have that desire in all that I am doing.
> I hope that I will never do anything apart from
> that desire.
>
> And I know that if I do this you will lead me by the right road,
> though I may know nothing about it.
> Therefore will I trust you always though
> I may seem to be lost and in the shadow of death.
>
> I will not fear, for you are ever with me,
> and you will never leave me to face my perils alone.[10]
>
> THOMAS MERTON

---

[9] Attrib. Edmund Burke

[10] The Merton Prayer from Thoughts in Solitude.

PANDEMIC 30.04.20

In times like these
Silence is the only answer.
There is no answer
to the self-seeking
self-aggrandisement,
self-serving that says
Everything is fine and
together we will beat this thing.

And the unskilled and the
foreigners and the poorly paid and the old
die.

There is no answer in the Silence.
Silence is the only answer – there is no question
to ask.

Silence is the only prayer there is…

THE KINDNESS OF STRANGERS

Out of the darkness
freed from fear
a stranger spoke
of separation and isolation and sickness.*

A baby pressed her face
to the window
and laughed with joy
to see her daddy enclosed inside.*

And the world hummed with life
and in that moment
I was not alone

and the Silence resonated with love.

---

*BBC South West News. 06.05.20

6 MAY

'...darkness may have significance. In it we each come face to face with our selves and our sinfulness. It is a road of repentance, metanoia, transformation...there is no arrival point... only a following...' [11]

Acknowledging my unpleasant, sometimes even downright nasty self is hard. It is not in me to be racist, violent or abusive – and yet sometime these vile things bubble up from some dank place and surface like marsh gas – if only in my thoughts. So I have to admit these thoughts *are* me. I am not always kind, patient and loving.

> There are many times when the thoughts surface without my bidding...
> "Do you have any idea what you look like?"
> "God, you're fat!"
> "Oh, I could smack you one!"
>
> All unthinkingly I make rapid assumption on appearance alone...
> "He's young, black and wearing hoodie, steer clear"
> "Look at her on her phone, ignoring her baby"
>
> The nastiness is endless, and I am ashamed of myself. How then do I learn to love this shadow self as God does?
>
> When we reach the bottom of all that we know we may find that we haven't reached the bottom at all – we've reached the centre.

---

[11] p1234 Celtic Daily Prayer Book 2

Enter Silence as entering
a cave, or a tomb
approach with trepidation
terror even.
Tiptoe into Silence's dark
recesses
pushing away the back bats
of fear
deaf to the drip, drip, drip
of consciousness –

go back, back, back.
You are a stranger here
no speech to tell you who you are,
where you are.
You are a foreigner in a foreign land.
There are no rights to claim
no wealth to take.
There is nothing you have
to offer.
Silence has nothing to give.
It is for we to give
our nothingness
to Silence.

Alone, today.
In pain for them,
for me.
Dreams shattered.
Hope turned to ashes.
Alone.
There is nothing left
to mend.
There is no future,
just past
might-have-beens.
Alone.
Again.
Each of us.
Isolated
in
our
separate
pain.

I am a tangled ball
of multicoloured wool played
with endlessly by a capricious kitten God.

Somewhere among the knots and threads,
warps and wefts and shifting shapes
are a beginning and an end –
a thread that will bring meaning and sense –
if only I can find it.

I must unravel my tangled multicoloured wool,
but I can't find the beginning
nor the end.

What will happen to my messy, tangled,
pretty ball of wool
if the kitten becomes bored
and runs away
to play with the leaves in the wind…

…will I then ever be fully woven?

"My house burned down. Now I can see the moon rising."
MIZUTA MASAHIDE, 17THC JAPANESE POET

Awake, longing for dawn…

Somewhere, deep, deep
inside
there is a song waiting
to be sung.
It cannot be summoned,
remembered, or
brought to mind
at will.

The song bubbles up
through the boggy ground
of the soul
like marsh gas
will-o'-the-wisp
just a word,
a phrase
a hint of a melody…

…then erupts,
Unbidden,
long forgotten.
'Silent night, holy night…
all is quiet all is calm…
sleep
in heavenly peace,
sleep in heavenly peace.'

WOOL-GATHERING IN A PANDEMIC

as a snake sheds its skin

as a lava becomes a dragonfly
as a chrysalis becomes a moth
as a tadpole becomes a frog
as a nut becomes a hazel bush
as a seed becomes an apple tree
as an acorn becomes an oak
as many grapes make wine
as many grains of wheat become a loaf of bread
so will I become...

all the doors have slammed shut, and I,
I am alone,
outside in the hallway,
the alleyway...

Anything that is capable of decaying is also capable of renewal and regeneration – it is sometimes called resurrection.

That's who I was...
an error, a mistake,
a shouldn't-have-happened.

That's who I was...
an absent daughter to a missing father
a failure at eleven, and sixteen
and twenty-two
and forty.

That's who I was...
a mother, a lover
a helper, a friend,
a Jill of all trades
and mistress of none.

That's who I was...
a divorcee, a scholar,
a teacher, a jam maker,
a farmer,
a soul companion.

That's who I was.

Then I got sick
and I do not know who I am anymore...

What if all this dying is really regeneration, resurrection?

I turned a corner...

and slammed into a brick wall.

I was expecting a different vista.
I was expecting – oh,
an alpine meadow, tall grasses
star-studded with wild flowers.

I was expecting gentle hills
crowned with oak and ash and maple
I was expecting pine forests,
mountains, blue with distance.

I was expecting the lazy soaring of buzzards
I was expecting the acrobatics
of swifts and swallows
and lark song filling the air.

What I got was another brick wall
and the thud, thud, thud of the jackhammer in my head.

The ground on which
I stand
is quicksand
shifting under my feet

bog-ridden
will-o-the-wisp
quaking
slithering...

to keep from sinking
I must move ever faster
there is no safe ground
only quicksand.

I look for comforting things
a reassuring word
a sentence in a book
a small miracle in a
dark day.

I tell myself stories
about a conflict
about a conversation
about a passing thought in a
dark mind.

I bury the wild, uncontrollable things
in the dark earth,
in the leaf-mould of my heart,
in the silt of my soul
and expect it to lie there, die there.

Of course, it does not. it grows.
And there is no controlling it.

"There are walks in which I lose myself, walks which return me to myself." [12]

LINDISFARNE

The poet said
"Traveller, there is no road;
...you make your own path as you walk"[13]
The Christ man said
"I am the Way,
...follow me".
And I don't know how.

I take my tired, sick body
and walk...

I walk the rabbit-bitten turf
the ground soft
beneath my blue suede boots.

I walk the rock-pebbled shoreline,
weight carefully placed on
unsteady surf strewn sea's debris.

I don't think. I don't remember.
I don't agonise. I don't pray.
At long, long last my chattering,
fearful, anxious
monkey-mind gives way

to my tired sick body
and allows it to heal and lead
and put its feet where it will...

and it does.

It remembers how to walk,
how to wobble and find its balance,
how to feel rough rock
and taste salt spray on lips
that spring from sea and eye.

---

[12] Thomas A Clark. 'In Praise of Walking'. 2016

[13] Antonio Machado. 1875-1939

It remembers how to see far horizons
and distant green shores,
new perspectives undistorted
by what is possible,

set free as the fulmars
and artic terns,
buffeted by unseen air streams
and unexpected sea currents –
felt, and carried along by forces
impossible to resist.

And the deep peace of the rolling wave
invades the heart and swamps the soul
and breath and life are restored.

"Traveller, there is no road; only a ship's wake on the sea"[14]

And so, I walk…

---

[14] ibid

Lost in a foreign landscape
wandering from oasis
to stream,
to shady copse
with no waymark understood –
and back again
retracing steps
as in a mirror
barely recognisable
and somehow familiar.

Broad plains stretch
away from sight toward
distant mountains where thunderheads gather
bruising their peaks
where the gentians and alpine flowers
fearfully crouch in crevasses
waiting, waiting, waiting
for the storm clouds to spend
listening, listening,
only listening
for the still small voice
whispering

– lost in a foreign landscape.

I enter the Silence
as entering an abandoned
house, derelict
eyeless windows, ivy-clung
no sound
of children's laughter
nor murmur of the kettle on the hob
singing to amuse itself
no tick, tocking
of the mantle clock
nor smell of fresh-baked bread
Just the mindless coo of pigeons
in the bare rafters
and shells of butterflies
trapped forever in sticky spider webs.

No one has been here for a long, long time.

Roaming around inside myself —
lost
unhappy dislocated I find
hidden treasures
in long forgotten crevices

I flip them over in my mind
I warm them in my hands
turning them over and over
marvelling at their iridescence
their heft their completeness

And then I let them go like
freeing
a butterfly from a windowpane

...and I am strangely comforted

The potter makes a space in the clay.
Where there is space
there is nothing
and in the nothingness of the space
in the clay
can be held apples and water,
and dreams...

Find the place where
the out-breath
becomes the in-breath

the pause,

the hiatus,

the space...

...before the in-breath
becomes the out-breath.

This is where you are.

This is where your soul spirit is permeable,
porous, liminal.

Go with the tide
the ebb and flow of it.
Let the storm of the high tide
leave the detritus of your life high
on the shoreline for the seabirds to pick over
and the scavengers to find what they will.

Let the little crabs scuttle back
and the drifting kelp lie still.
You will retreat to the sea's womb,
to that deep ocean's place pulled by the moon
and, gathering strength,
you will once again
fling yourself into the arms of the welcoming shore,
drenched by foaming spume that cleans
and makes of every pebble and grain of sand
a bright jewel.

DREAM

I find a girl-child
in the place where I am happy.
She is new here
in her best clothes
sharply pressed.
I take her under my wing.
"Come with me" I say,
"You will love it here."
We pause by the new lake
where rowdy boy-childs
are hurling rocks, disturbing
the wildfowl
the serenity...
a crowd gathers
and begins to run towards
us
I stand still in my space
and the crowd rushes by.
I am ignored
and I have lost the girl-child.

Who do you consider I am? Female, certainly. White – I suppose, although I do wonder who my parents', parents' parents were... British by nationality and birth although my DNA says differently. Christian – culturally and nominally. Society and income say I am middle-class, a tidy blanket that covers a multitude of sins. And I am retired – though from what I'm not certain. So there you have it. I am British, white, female, middle-class, retired, and old. That ticks the boxes. That's me pigeon-holed.

Think again!

All you, and I, can say with any certainty is that I am a human being. One of nearly eight billion other human beings. We all breathe the same air. That's it. That's what unites us. That's what puts us in a pigeon-hole. As a human being, nearly eight billion other human beings are my sisters and brothers, parents and grandparents, children.

We are a family of human beings. When we hurt each other we hurt all our family. When we have compassion for each other we have compassion for all our family.

We are human, capable of being hurt and hurting but we are also capable of loving kindness and compassion and love. That makes us who we are – one in nearly eight billion human beings, each unique and uniquely loved. We breathe the same air, and our one common goal is to seek happiness and avoid suffering. Why then can we not live in peace together?

IMAGINE A GOD MADE IN OUR OWN IMAGE...

A God who looks like us.
A womanly God
a manly God
a God with ginger hair and crooked teeth.

A God with black scarred skin
and bare feet.
A God with beautiful eyes
and cheekbones like broad plains.

Imagine a God
strong shouldered
propelling her wheelchair
a God who runs on blades,
a competitive God,
a God who depends on drugs
just to get through the day.

Imagine a God who looks like us –
in all our infinite variety
and beauty.

Every day, every dawning
every risen morning
every eye-opening
comes resurrection.

Death has called time for now,
night's terrors and slumberous sleep
are gone
beyond change and done with.

The sun's rising brings a new breath
a new blessing, a new promise.

Today is a new day that hasn't been fucked up yet.[15]

Breathe in this new day
with all its promise
and hope
resurrection comes with the daily dawning.
And it hasn't been fucked up yet.

---

[15] Written in the dirt on the back of a container lorry cab.

PRODIGAL DAUGHTER

Sometimes in prayer
God and I talk – mostly
I talk
and God listens.

Occasionally,
in a lull in the conversation
God will speak words of love
and wisdom and I listen.

Usually, in prayer
I talk, am silent, wait,
and God is busy elsewhere.

I pray
I plead, I beg,
I cry,
but God is absent.

I pray some more.
I get angry.
How am I so worthless
that God doesn't bother to show up?

I ask and I ask and I ask
and you
you do not answer.
You are messing with my head
God.
Why? What have I ever done to you?

Not good enough for you, eh?

Looking for God is about as useless as a fish in the sea looking for the ocean.

PARABLE.

Not so long ago, in a place close by, there was a woman who had two daughters. She was a single smother who had done well for herself. She owned much property of many kinds and made a good living for herself and her daughters.

Not very long ago at all, the younger of the daughters went to her mother and said "Mum, it's lovely here but I want to live my own life. I feel stifled here, I want to travel and meet new people and taste new food and go to exiting places." So the mother, with a heavy heart did what her daughter asked and divided up all the property and gave her her share of it. And a few days later the young woman gathered up all her belongings and set off for lands unknown without so much as a backward glance.

She had a wonderful time. She drank fine wines, ate rich food and lavished her money on haute couture clothes, new friends and the designer drugs of the moment. And the sex was amazing! She really knew how to live it up. But the day came when the money ran out. And as the money ran out, so did her friends. A recession due to climate change, government mismanagement and war overtook that place and she began to be very frightened. She was homeless, penniless and friendless. She got a job washing dishes in a greasy spoon café. She would have gladly eaten the food from the dirty plates but there rarely was any.

And then came a morning, after sleeping perilously in a shop doorway, when she at last came to her senses. "Even my mother's cleaners and gardeners and maintenance people have enough to eat and somewhere safe to sleep at night. But here I am without anything to eat and in danger of being beaten up or worse. I will leave now and go to my mother and beg her forgiveness for being so selfish and ungrateful and I'll ask her for a job working nights in security or cleaning her offices or mowing the grass around her estates. So off she set, hoping against hope that her mother would not disown her and send her away.

And while she was still a long way from home her mother got news of her and was so overjoyed at the return of her lost daughter that she got in her Aston Martin DB6 and rushed off to meet her. She was so filled with love and compassion for her daughter when she saw her that she jumped out of the car and hugged and kissed her. Her daughter said "Mum, I have been so stupid. I took all you gave me and threw it away and now I have nothing. I'm so ashamed but if you let me, I'll work for you as a servant and try to pay you back."

Her mother said nothing but took out her phone and rang home to the housekeeper. "I'm bringing my daughter home" she said "Quickly, bring out some clothes, the best you can find – and get out jewellery, rings, and necklaces, oh, and shoes for her feet. And tell the chef to whip up a feast! This daughter of mine was lost and has now come home!" And so the party began...

Meanwhile, the eldest daughter had been at work all day, overseeing the family business and when she came home, worn out and ready to put her feet up and be quiet, she heard music and dancing and laughter and chatter. She called over the housekeeper and asked what was happening. The housekeeper replied "Your sister has come home and your mother has laid on this wonderful party because she's back safe and sound."

The elder sister was so angry. She refused to join in the fun and so their mother came out to call her in. But she said to her mother, "Come in! You must be joking. Ever since she's left, I've worked hard for you, day in and day out. I have done everything you asked me to do but you've never put on a party like this so I could celebrate with my friends. But this daughter of yours, who has spent all your money living the high life and done goodness knows what, you, you've laid on the finest food and drink for her!"

The mother replied, "Daughter, you are always with me, and I love you more than you will ever know. What is mine is yours. But we just had to celebrate and be overjoyed, because this sister of yours was dead and has come to life, she was lost and has come home."

> 'Many small people, who in many small places do many small things, can alter the face of the world'[16]

'Do small things with great love', said Mother Teresa. Jesus told of small things — a widow's mite, mustard seeds, sparrows, hair on heads, a drink of water, a few loaves and fishes, breadcrumbs under the table… Humility lies in understanding that most of us can only do small things. Most of us are not the earth shakers, the policy makers, the change brokers, we are too small — one in nearly eight billion. And it feels hopeless to even try. And yet, and yet — we do try. Often, we fail. Our plans turn to ashes, our good intentions become unnoticed dust under other people's feet. Sometimes, even when we succeed, no-one notices. Our good deeds are ignored, our kind actions go unrecorded and even our heroic moments vanish seconds later. And no-one knew that all this goodness stemmed from our being a Christian, or a Muslim, or a Jew, or a Sikh, or a Hindu or a Humanist, or indeed, a human being. And it's not fair, is it?

Well, actually it is. How many times have each of us been helped by a smile, a phone call, an encounter, that came at exactly the right time? Did we notice? Did we know, or care, who that person, animal, lake, sunset was? I doubt it. All we knew was that suddenly, or gradually, our hearts lifted, our sorrow dissipated, and the world seemed a better place. And we probably went on our way, rejoicing.

And when asked "Where is your God?", don't give me "God is in that situation and God is crying too". God may well be crying, crying with anger and frustration at good people's apathy and good people's greed. Now, who was it said, "Where were you when I was hungry and in prison?" Hmm?

We need to stop trying to read the mind of God. It's a good strategy for avoiding what we don't want to do. The words that strike fear into my heart are *"God told me what to do."* Doesn't that just sound like Adam's *'the woman told me to do it'*? It usually means, *'I want to do this so I'm certain it's what God wants too.'* We must learn the poverty of no reward, no thanks, no praise. We do not have to know outcomes, we do not have to be thanked — although that is nice too — all we need to know is, that whatever the action, we made someone's or something's life better, for that moment. Being Christ in the world is what we are called to be (if we're Christian, that is. Other faiths and no faiths have their impetus too, just as sacred, just as loving…) Mother Teresa told her nuns, *"I don't want you to preach about Jesus — I want you to be Jesus."* Precisely.

---

[16] African proverb written on the Berlin Wall

CREDO

Some of you, my friends and family will know that for some time I have had an ongoing problem with faith. I believe utterly in following in the footsteps of Jesus, and sometimes I follow St Francis' example too. I believe utterly in doing my very best to be Christ in the world in all its bigness and littleness. I accept that I mostly fail.

I renounce utterly all forms of Christianity that rejects others on *any* grounds whatsoever. I renounce all forms of violence, especially those done in the name of God. I reject the domination and violence, however subtle and supposedly justified, done to women, LGBT+ people, Black people, Asian people, differently abled people, people of other faiths and humanist people.

I reject the violence done to this planet, our home and our mother, in the name of expedience and profit. Where all these are perpetuated in the name of Christianity, I renounce and reject them.

I announce my aspiration to follow the way of solidarity with all of creation and humanity as taught by Jesus and by Francis.

I know now that I do not have a faith problem or a Christianity problem. I have a Church problem.

It is OK to do something just because you want to, to do the thing that someone has told you you cannot. Overstep the boundaries – that is what they are for. Just remember – you do not have to go to church – just *be* the church.

> 'Only those who will risk going too far can possibly find out how far one can go.'
> T S ELIOT

Turn aside
and stop
and look...
What *was* that?
A rainbow in a puddle,
a sparrow learning how to fly,
A glimpse of glory caught in a spider's web?

Turn aside
and stop
and wait.
Take off your shoes.
On what holy ground are you treading?

Turn aside...
for in muddy puddles
in windswept hollows, in fallen leaves
lies your treasure

and you must give all you have to possess it.

Step off the path, Mortal.
Where is it that
is so important for you to go?

Get off the well-worn track of tired religion,
stumble into the wilderness,
the briars and the blackthorn.

Better here
than the way that is known.
Better this way, than that.

I am the Way
and in the wilderness angels minister
and briars and blackthorn bear bitter-sweet fruit.

Step off the path, Mortal
step off the path
and step onto the Ground of my Being.

Sink to the bottom
and there you will find
all the silt and detritus
of your life, all the muck
and the filth of your living.

And you can curl up
and lie in the swamp of it.
You can become
foetus-like in the dark womb
of your doubt.

And then, in your misery

will you realise
that the silt and the swamp
and the darkness
of the womb
is the seedbed watered by your tears
and fertilized by your despair.

In the silence
in the noise
in the rush
in the quiet
in the stilling
be my seeing where I need to see
be my hearing where I need to hear
be my touching where I need to touch.

If I am touched, give me grace
to question
to listen
to change
to die a little more
to heal a little more
until the work of weaving is done
and all is finished.

I sit at your feet
waiting
as a wood anemone sits
at the feet of a mighty oak.

What does a small, fragile flower
know of a sturdy, gnarled oak?

It is there – for sure
it throws an awesome shadow
but measuring the height, width,
breadth and depth of it

is beyond imagination
beyond thought
beyond words

I sit among the detritus
of roots and twigs and leaves
and earth – and wait.

All my life, so far, I realise that I have wanted to please, to fit in, to be liked and I have tailored my living to meet those expectations of others. Why did I not listen to the deep unease within me? Why did I have to get to a place of physical dis-ease before I acknowledged how accommodating I had been? My body ached. Locked in, I had restricted movement. Was I using my body as a metaphor? I was stiff-necked, my hips hurt, and my shoulders were carrying an unseen load. The doctor called it fibromyalgia. I beg to differ.

Enough then I did not want to fit into some male notion of Church. God is not 'he' and I am not called to be like 'him' nor worship 'him'. Time was when gods were male and female. But that will never do. So now it is time to reclaim or re-imagine God as neither male nor female. God is too small and made in our own image, idolatry surely, when we insist on naming the Holy One 'he', 'king', 'lord'?

To be born female is to be born 'other than'; other than the original and best, a poor sort of copy of the Maker's original idea. A hastily cobbled-together 'help-mate' when the original complained of loneliness. Someone to blame, bear the children and do the donkeywork. And so it still is. Men are born with the memory of being the original model for what is right and human. They may not all have wanted the power and mindset, but they have it, and they use it. Women know, deep down, that they are an addition. The Bible tells them so. But then the Bible was written by men so afraid of their own power and accountability that they needed women to blame when things went wrong. *"She made me do it. She tempted me."* Whatever was God thinking?

So insidious is the male persona in religion that we cease to notice it. Why is Jesus 'Lord' and 'King' when all he stood for according to the Gospels was to the least and lowest? Is our language so poor that we cannot find better epithets than the ones of war and male hierarchy?

Before we can tell other women of the denial of our female/feminine self we have to know it for ourselves. We have come into a world, into a faith tradition, that for millennia has believed women to be inferior. It is a tradition soaked in an authoritarian attitude that devalues, diminishes, and rejects women and the way in which they think and act.

This is dangerous thinking. How do you overturn thousands of years of 'Daddy knows best'? Think of the basics of any major religion. There is a male deity in charge, at the head. I can only speak with authority on the religion I have grown up with – Christianity, and then only a very small section of it. The first thing you learn is, 'Our Father...'. Any attempt at 'Our Mother...' is ridiculed. My attempt at 'Our Parent...' was met with *'Oh, you're one of those, are you?'*, with all its contemptuous connotations of strident females who might be dismissed on the grounds that they are probably lesbians. So women learn to be silent. In God's name, what is wrong with 'Holy One, who is in heaven...'? But there, we mustn't go around destroying men's image of the God they made in their own image.

Patrick, (not his real name) an elderly Irishman, occasionally used to wander by mistake, usually having downed a few, into the church where I was minister. Often this was during a service so I would be wearing my clerical collar. "Good morning, Father!" Patrick would yell, because being a Catholic, how could I be anything else if I were wearing a collar? We loved Patrick. His Catholic parish priest, another elderly Irishman, would speak to me if I weren't wearing my collar, just to say 'Hello'. If I was wearing it he ignored me. He quite literally did not see me. A female, wearing a clerical collar, just did not compute. We loved him too. But not as much as Patrick and his cheery "Good Morning Father!".

Women have unknowingly, unthinkingly, lovingly even, given away their wisdom and sacred power. We have been belittled out of it, bullied out of it, shamed out of it and it is time to take it back and reclaim what is rightfully ours. Not to take what is male spirituality and male power that is ill fitting. That has been tried and found wanting. Women must claim what is *theirs* to claim. Their sacredness and wisdom are part of the wholeness of God. Without women and men claiming, acknowledging, their immense power, finding their own spirituality in the soul of God is never going to be complete.

> Womanspace
> Move over,
> hutch up
> make room for us women.
>
> Move over you
> in the church
> in the cathedral, in the home.
> Space Invader.
>
> Shove up you
> in the boardroom,
> the factory floor, the racetrack.
> Ceiling-sealer.
>
> This is our space
> We are womanspreading
> shove over, hutch up, move along now
> make room for womansplaining...

'This is the final revelation of the mystery, the Father (sic) revealing his (sic) Self to the world and communicating his (sic) Spirit, and this Self and this Spirit are Love.' [17]

What if this was not the final revelation of the Great Mystery? Might it be – with the greatest of respect to Bede Griffiths who in no small way opened my eyes – that we should not assume that God could only perform the miracle that was Jesus, just the once? Perhaps we should not assume that Jesus was the pinnacle of God's ability and after that God sits back and lets the rest of us inadequate mortals get on with it knowing that we can never attain Christhood. Does that really sound like God to you? Does not every small act of Love form into a larger Christ as each small cell in the body builds into the larger being? Is this not a meaning of being part of the body of Christ? Love calls to love. Love calls to hate. This is resurrection. And Christ does not solely belong to Christians.

---

[17] Return to the Centre'. Bede Griffiths. p60.

Beyond the Vedas, the Sutras,
the Bible, the Koran...
beyond all these and more, lies Truth.
No one holds all the Truth —
persuade as they might try.

The Great Mystery runs
underground through all these
and more
like spoors, like fungi
and bacteria infecting,
connecting, rooting,
spreading
the revelation of Truth.

It whispers in the treetops
shouts down the canyons and mountain crags
'There is more than you can ever know'

Do not be satisfied with what you see,
you are told, you know.
Dive deeply into your inner Ground,
your Earth, your humus, your seed bed

your heart-like womb, and there,
in the place called Silence is where Truth may be spoken...

Mystery abides and Wisdom breathes
her honied breath.

What if Gaia is the one you call God?

EVERYTHING

everything –
every living thing
every thing that exists
rock, amoeba, celandine,
grasshopper, lynx,
sparrow, toad and child
has its place
its space
its intrinsic value
in
and for
itself
interrelated
and
interconnected
part of the web of life.

The Great Holy.
Sacred.

IT ALL BEGINS WHEN I TURN ASIDE...

Soul places,
where the within us
reaches out
to the without us.
Where yearnings we did not know were there,
touch the Infinite.

Soul places,
reaching out into the beyond
to taste the honeyed cream of
forgotten life
half-remembered as in a vision
or a dream.

Soul places,
where earth and sea meet
sky and heaven holds its
breath
and a Mortal sighs
with the joy of homecoming.

In a clearing in the forest
Silence dwells.
Dark, stern trees surround
the empty space
nothing dares grow in their shade.

In the clearing in the forest
Silence dwells
scarcely noticing the wood anemone
nor the hart's tongue fern.
It is daring enough they are there.

Do not dare to boldly
enter Silence.
Let Silence, like a small
shy, wild beast
creep slyly, unbidden
to your side.

Do not dare to grasp
Silence
and attempt to bind it
to your will.
Silence has sharp teeth
and you will be left bleeding...

> 'If you are out of balance, take inspiration from manifestations of your true nature.'[18]

Good it would be to take inspiration from manifestations, sight-seeings of your True Self.

Is the True Self the Will o' the Whisp
that drifts across the high moors
exulting in the combes and drifts and barren nakedness?

Is the True Self the watcher
by the seashore,
knees to chin on the rocks, guarding eternity?

Is the True Self the word on the wind
whispering,
repent, rethink, return?

Who are you, O mortal to imagine such things?

I am who I AM.
I am who you made me.
Will you deny me wholeness?

---

[18] Jean Yves Leloup. 'The Gospel of Mary Magdelene. 2002. p65

It is the presence I am missing.
I know it's there
everything outside and inside tells me so
violets, sedge, ripe plums,
rain, wrens and whales,
feverfew

random things tell me
so... inspire

awe, wonder, thankfulness
roll over me
like a fresh wind on a hot day
but I do not deep down
sense the Presence.

Like a fish in the ocean
looking for water

I seek and I do not find.

I have miles to go before I sleep.

Poetry is me expressing myself to the Other. It is my way of articulating my fears, anxieties, anger, frustration – and love. Inadequate as it is, my poetry gives me a language and expression that is denied in everyday language. Poems and poetry are my alter-language, my burning bush, bright field, pond where the wood duck sleeps.

Poems are my prayers, psalms, laments and celebrations of creation. Poetry is my song, my speaking in tongues, my logos, my kairos – my voice. Poetry is Sophia, Ruach, the wind in the trees whose only sign of passing is the bowing of branches and the love sigh of the leaves.

Poetry, in the final analysis (if one should indeed analyse poetry – I think not), should speak for itself as does a great painting, or landscape. Poetry is self-offering, sacrifice – sacrament even. One stands on holy ground and can do no other.

> Elusive God.
> Would you ever just stand
> still
> a moment and wait for me
> to catch up…
>
> …But no.
> I pause for breath,
> to drink in the sea
> to bathe in your creation
> and there you are –
>
> Gone, again.

I cannot rid myself of the picture of God being the grey-haired old man in a nightshirt a la Sistine Chapel. The one who seems to me to be pointing a finger at humanity, and me, and saying 'You are guilty'. Thank you, La Sainte Union Convent for that fear-inducing, soul-shrivelling image.

My mind rejects utterly that image. My body remembers it, deep down where I cannot reach, and shudders. Somehow, that image is so deeply intrenched into my heart and soul that just the word 'God' conjures up the punishing, abusive old man who doesn't love me because I am unlovable.

I sense that somewhere out there, in here, is a Source. A source of energy, a beating pulse, a web of life, benevolent intelligence, a unity of mystery and meaning. But I don't know how to connect to it. I don't know if I even *can* connect to it. I need to rid myself of that awful old man.

> You white men
> do not have God's authority
> to do what you do.
>
> Saying you have does not
> make it so.
>
> 'There is no authority except
> that which God has established'
> you say.
>
> But who says God gave it
> to you?
>
> I say God gave it to us,
> women, children – any
> minorities, anyone
> at all who is not white male.
>
> So, white male, ask yourself
> what are you doing to God
> and under whose authority?

God – if such a thing
exists
does not need your protection.

God does not need you
to defend the name of God
or fly to God's defence.

God does not need you
to prove
God exists.

God doesn't need you
in a building
worshipping the name of God
on Sundays or any other day

those are your little needs.

God – if such a thing exists

needs to love you.

It seems to me that I have spent much of my life looking for a father so I could be a dutiful daughter. Where on earth did I get this idea from? Having no father figure except an authoritarian Victorian grandfather, who, it must be said, I adored, but who ruled his daughters with a rod of iron, I realise now I have spent my life unknowingly looking for a 'father' I don't need. Like Pavlov's dogs we have been rewarded by men in authority when we become, behave, like dutiful daughters. When we step out of line, we are ridiculed, put down, punished, shown our place.

Religious institutions are institutions that are and have been, created by men for men. The only role for women is that of 'helpmeet', server, servant. Oddly, that is the role Jesus took.

I expect to get attacked for these ideas of mine, but, more probably, I shall be ignored. That's how religion keeps women in line. For sure there are now women bishops in the Anglican Church, (and women Moderators in the URC have long been evident). But with what grudgingness and at what cost to their femaleness? In order to be who they are, women have had to become 'men'. They may not think that they have, they may be thinking that they have arrived on their own terms. They are wrong. In order to conform, they dress like their male counterparts, they act like their male counterparts – their congregations and their culture demand it. And so, again, all the good things that women could bring to the table, their intuition, their imagination, their inspiration, are denied and that is a loss. Every time a woman goes to church she is subliminally reminded that she is second best. 'Our Father...' is preferred to 'Our Parent', and 'Our Mother...' is never heard. All things are done 'in the name of the Father...'. And many priests are designated 'Father' by their peers and their congregations. If God is 'Father', what are these men saying about themselves?

Women have not entered the hierarchy of the Church on female terms – that is not good enough. They have been allowed to enter on male terms, because as far as anyone can see, those are the *only* terms possible. There is no other way. Except of course, there is. There is Jesus' way. His way of equality and healing and sacrifice and love for neighbour and God. It's all there, in the Gospels if only you take time to look.

Is it that, deep down, men are afraid of women, of women claiming their fair share? Maybe it goes further, maybe women might claim more than their fair share. Women might take away men's power and authority, men's right to view the world and its structures through purely masculine eyes. And they must believe this because this is what they do. (I would like to add, that this is not true of all men. But I will not because those who do hold this view will automatically assume that they are one of those that do not. They don't have the ability to think in any other way.)

What would our institutions, our world look like through feminine/female eyes? Where would men's place be in that world? And not just women's eyes, but LGBT+ eyes, and differently abled eyes. Therein lies the fear. There is an unknown, unordered land where the Wild Goose could fly where she wills.

GOOD FRIDAY - ANY YEAR

They're doing it again
God,
they're doing it again.

You'd think once would be enough
God,
but no, they're doing it again.

They are crucifying in Gaza
and Israel
in Sudan and Myanmar,

They are crucifying in Ukraine,
and there will be more in Rwanda soon
if the powerful ones have their way,

those ones who party while others
mourn, or choose between eating
and warmth.

They are doing it again
God,
and the poor wait on
resurrection...

Doubt has been my travelling companion for many years. Does God exist? Is there really life after death? Is there any point to anything? In case you think this is some form of depression, let me hasten to say I believe in a benevolent Universe. I believe in Original Blessing, and I believe in a Holy One, the Source of my Being. I believe in a Creator who continually re-creates and co-creates with us.

I have in the past followed a well-worn map. It shows hills and valleys, lanes and motorways. Its contour lines and dotted footpaths are familiar to me, its boundaries known. Now, somehow, without almost noticing, I've fallen off the edge of my map.

Doubt and I wander in an uncharted land. We do not recognise the territory and there are no known landmarks. Yet we are not lost, we are not frightened. We walk like wondering children, hand in hand, and know that we are safe, even when Doubt and I doubt that we can be. We have a lodestone that goes with us, and we are walking home, strangers in a strange land.

Doubt and I are good friends and comfortable travelling companions.

> Having climbed the mountain range
> of doubt
> the icy snow-clad peaks
> are reached at last
> bitter winds eddying like
> turbulent seas flatten
> the exhausted body
> against the jagged rocks and
> fills the eyes with tears that blind.
>
> But, it is a victory
> the flag is driven into barren rock.
>
> A hollow victory
> and a tattered flag...
>
> ...there, on the far receding horizon
> lies another Omolangma to climb[19]

---

[19] Local Tibetan name for Mt Everest

If I am not a Christian, what am I? Christened and confirmed in Church of England churches, educated, if that's the right word, in a Catholic convent, and married in a United Reformed Church.

My ministerial education was at an ecumenical Anglican college and my post-degree at Mansfield College Oxford, and sometimes Regent's College which was Baptist. I am also a Third Order Franciscan. If all that's not got a flavour of Christianity, then I don't know what I am. Off the Christian road map that's for sure. And yet Christian teachings have shaped my thoughts, my understanding of my world, and most of all, my moral compass.

It is that compass that has led me on my journeying and away from Church. I can see, in the distance, across a vast desert, the grandeur of the monolithic fortress of Christianity. I can see its castellations of certainty to be climbed, its sharp stones of dogma on which the unwary will skin their hands and knees. I can see the climbers and their sherpas all roped together the better to be safe from deviation. I can see it all – but I am not one of them.

Faith is not a fortress where the drawbridge of uncertainty can be pulled up. Faith is a journey. It is said that the longest journey begins with the first step. And that step is a step into the unknown and the uncharted. Here be dragons.

I am disappointed in you
God
you have failed me
again
you have left me to face
the night-time terrors
alone
again.

I am more than disappointed in you
God.
I am angry and disillusioned.
Love?
Don't make me laugh.

I am not Sarah.

Repentance is creative, remorse destructive.
I am always one step
behind you.

Most of the time
I think – or rather, don't think
but am
one step ahead of you
not knowing how out of step with you
I am.

Then you wait for me
and I catch up and match
the rhythm of your stride for a while.

How I long to always be
in step and to join in the dance.

Academia and I fell out. Although if I am honest I did not fit the mould of passive student and was flicked off as one would flick off an irritating fly.

I could not, and cannot, see why I should write in a style that is not my own, a style agreed by some long dead male academics and reinforced by the still living ones. I agree that ideas, writings, readings, theories not my own must be acknowledged and attributed. But just as every scientist, theologian, poet, artist and musician is recognised by their style and individuality, why not the academic writer?

It may be, or course, that I am just too untidy an intellectual, too messy a thinker. It may be that my sentences are too long, my style, as one long-ago lecturer put it, "too journalistic", but that is the poet in me struggling to get out.

I read with much envy, but some feeling of betrayal, books by Nicola Slee, Susan Durber, Paula Gooder..., who say so much of what I want to say, but in a form that is acceptable to the hallowed halls. Of course, what I write may be so much dross. I have, in mitigation, achieved a first degree and several widely differing modules of a Masters, so maybe not.

My besetting sin is I chase hares. I read a book and that book leads me to read several more, and several more and my thinking morphs into something else. My quarrel with the patriarchal Church's use of the word 'Father' led me to feminist writers, which led me to Liberation Theology and LGBT+ and Black Theology, and on to Black Feminist Theology. In time I found Ecology Theology and Creation Theology which reawakened my interest and curiosity in First Nations,[20] which is where my exploration of 'other than' and spiritualty first began. I wasted many years abandoning this curiosity as I was told by a Christian, well-meaning no doubt, that this was pagan and if I persisted only hell and damnation awaited.

I am truly grateful for those women and men who do their research, write their papers, struggle with their findings and publish their work. Without them I would be the poorer. But I cannot 'be' them. I can ape their methods and stick to their academic rules but my living inspiration becomes a dead thing, a dissected frog pinned to a board and no matter how much I poke it it will not jump. Academia is not my mother tongue.

---

[20] Specifically, Native American and the art of Australian Aboriginals.

MENDIPS

Why, to my eye
my self, my being,
are these barren
sheep-bitten fields
so breath-taking?

Why, with their secret caverns,
and holes and dens,
their rocky outcrops
and stunted thorny trees
that stumble across the landscape
do they fill my heart with joy?

Why, with the big sky draped
across their shoulders,
with their fog-mantle,
their slanting rain,
their utter, utter bleakness,
do they make my soul sing?

What coarse woollen thread
weaves together cave dweller,
ancient Celt, Roman industrialist,
tinker, packman, miner,
farmer, sojourner,
shaggy goats, scrawny sheep
and feral toad-eyed ponies?

Hold on to the thread –
it is the yarn of enduring,
belonging, hefting…
and will bring you home
if you but follow it,
weave with it,
wrap yourself in it.

There are no places
that become sacred
and we do not make them so
by placing statues
and plaques
and cairns
and crosses in the landscape.

These places have always
been sacred,
these hills and valleys,
these groves and springs
and we desecrate them with
our little attempts
at sacredness.

Look to the giants of
Easter Island,
Mount Rushmore,
Stonehenge
and weep.

Their creators meant well.

Wind-hover
wind lover
perfectly poised,
oblivious to my presence
fully fixated,
a keen eye on the rocks and crevices below
her outstretched, quivering wings suspended
in the turbulent air until, effortlessly
she veers away
across the winterfilled fields.

It is not given to me
to rejoice
in chalice and paten,
in wafer and wine
in dull-intoned words
and soaring song.

My Holy Communing
is spread before me,
a feast, a banquet
daily, in everchanging sky
in rocky fields
where grow violets and cowslips
thistles and nettles,
Tom Thumb and wild thyme.

And daily, like the skylark
buzzard, rook and
red kite
my soul takes wings
and soars…

MENDIP HILLS - KINGSDOWN

This windswept, icy place,
with wide, windswept skies
is not a destination
but rather, a resting space.

There is no call to do anything,
just to be present.
To be still, to achieve nothing,
to expect nothing.

It is the place, space,
between breaths...
It is the interlude before the music begins
again and the dance goes on.

DAWN

Slate grey streaks
of clouds
showing their pink underbelly,
striated by silver sky
reveal pony silhouettes
breakfasting
on the sheep-nibbled, windswept hill.
Another day dawns...

Loose the chains that bind
to ponderous, clinging earth
cut the bonds,
set free the heavy body burden
and let the soul soar
skywards –

set free the wild goose within.

Jesus was a Jew. It might seem obvious to point this out but he was a man with olive skin and dark hair. He had all the physical and mental characteristics of his race. He spoke in Aramaic, a Semitic language. He defined himself through his culture and community and could only think of God in relation to the Jewish Scripture of his day. And yet, time and again, he referred to himself as the Word of God, as being sent by God, as being one with God. From where did these words arise? How did he dare to voice his innermost thoughts?

So... if we can only express ourselves in English (or Yiddish or Urdu or Mandarin Chinese) and we can only think of ourselves and God (or Jehovah or Allah or Krishna or....) in terms of the Bible (or the Koran, or the Tanakh or Guru Granth Sahib or ...), may we not be allowed to know in the depths of our souls, in the ground of our being, beyond words and thoughts to be the Word of God, one with the Great Mystery, one with the Holy Spirit? Is that blasphemous? I don't think so. We are not Jesus the Christ. We strive to be like him, to love like him, to serve like him, to lay down our lives for others like him. And some of us do it very much better than others. Like Mother Teresa, like Martin Luther King, like Mahatma Gandhi, like Bede Griffiths, like Richard Rohr, like Matthew Fox, like the Dalai Lama, like Desmond Tutu, like all the unnamed women who stand up to patriarchy and get slapped down, like all those thousands of ordinary people who fight against racism and suffer hatred and abuse, like those who are LGBT+ and their friends who have been hounded out of their places of worship.

Most of us just do the best we can – and sometimes not even that. But we carry on, because we are all part of the Lexicon of God and together we are the Word – whatever and wherever that is.

They drew a circle that shut us out
Heretics, rebels, things to flout.
But love and we had the wit to win;
We drew a circle and took them in!

EDWIN MARKHAM, 1852-1940

The monster is unleashed –
and no one has noticed.
It is prowling the world destroying.
It causes freshwater lakes to become saline,
to dry up.

It strides the world in seconds infecting
young minds holding out
glittering prizes of celebrity, airbrushed beauty,
Warhol's fifteen minutes...

It creates need where there is none
and the want and the need are boredom
and thrown away. They fill the oceans
and the oceans' offspring. And their bodies make new islands
bobbing in response.

It starts wars where there was peace
in the name of democracy. It hits out before it is hit
because deep down the monster is terrified
of looking inward

at the monster it has created of itself.

The Monster has a name. Lookinwardanddeny.

I look to the hills
and there is no help.

I look to my God
and there is none.

*Look deeply inside yourself,
there your help will be.*

And I look and there is no help,
just a deep bottomless pit.

*My God, my God
why have you forsaken me?*

THE EMPEROR'S NEW CLOTHES

Faith shifting
shape shifting
believe in what you
believe
question the Law
become a faith shifter
become
a dissenter,
a heretic.
If you must,
become a prophet.

They will not thank you
for muddying the waters
of their certainties
but somewhere in the silt
are the caddis flies of Truth.

Faith sifting...

IT'S A GIRL!

Christ the woman – born a girl-child,
has been missing presumed dead
for many a century.

She has always been there – of course overshadowed,
relegated to dark corners and dusty vestries
or paganised and discounted.

Now, the girl-child is reborn – re-cognised.
She is seen (for those with eyes to see)
in Rosie, in Jackie, in Corinne

And Pauline and Alice and Julie – times two.
In Nicola and Marcella, in Matthew and Richard and Maya
and Ed and Wendell.

She is born again – in Lucy and Sue and Yvonne
She is here in Richard and Rob and Stephen
and Ian and you and me.

Christ, the girl-child – born this day
and this, and this…born to live and learn,
to teach and heal and be crucified.

Always, being born – rising again
Christa, Woman, stranger, incognito, unexpected.
God's Anointed.

If I disagree with you, that doesn't make you my enemy. Nor am I yours. I disagree with you – that's all. You do not have to agree with me. I will do you the courtesy of assuming that whatever it is we disagree on, you have thought about, questioned. I trust that you will do me the same courtesy. When I disagree with you I am not implying that I am right and you are wrong. I am saying that I see this thing differently. You are not my enemy.

I am not rubbishing your beliefs, nor what you have been taught. Tell me about this, talk to me, I really want to know. Perhaps you would like to know my beliefs and teachings. Perhaps not. Either way, we can continue to disagree, and we will not be enemies.

RESOLUTION

'Let the beauty we love be what we do'

RUMI[21]

I will be a Christian
who doesn't go to church.

I will be a believer who doesn't believe
in God the Father and handed-down male hierarchy

I will be a follower of a 1st century Jew and will not
be a follower of shabby, worn-out Christianity.

I will be a guardian of creation
not a keeper of doctrine and liturgy.

I will be thankful and share what I have
and mourn those I lose along the Way because

I will be a Christian who doesn't go to church.
I will love them when they turn away.

I will not make enemies of them.

---

[21] Jalal ad-Din Muhammad ar-Rumi. Sufi mystic and poet 1207-1273

Come as you are
you don't have to put on
a smile, a mask, new clothes
you don't have to wash
your face, your body, your hands
you don't have to look
good or neat and tidy.

Come as you are
with all your grubby nastiness
your petty foibles
your sins
your deep-down hatefulness
your disbelief,
your scorn
you're not perfect, don't even try.

Just come as you are
because you're loved – as you are.

ORTHODOX HERESY

Amo, amas, amat
amamus, amatis, amant.
I love, you love,
he, she or
it loves...

What 'it' loves?
What is 'it' that loves me, you
him, her and they?
It loves...

I am so slow to catch up.
So slow learning
how (not)[22] to speak of God.

I tilt at the windmills
of Father, Himself, King, Lord...

...and time and again
am knocked from my high horse.

Mother, Herself, Queen
from lack of giving tongue
are awkward misborn misfits.
And Goddess will never do.

What then emerges?
What is left?
It does.
It emerges.
'It' is all there is.

It cannot be named, labelled, cosied up to...
Easier to pick up mercury...

...Amat.

---

[22] How (Not) To Speak of God. Peter Rollins 2006. SPCK

I dreamt that my bag was stolen, and I was in a foreign place with no means of support. I was given money but no help at all. I had been talking to a young refugee woman with a child in a buggy. Had she stolen my bag? Why would I think it was she who stole from me? What kind of person am I that thinks such things?

> What has been stolen from me?
> What must I give birth to
> to replace that which was valuable –
> stolen from me?
>
> Essence, that's what.
> The 'who I am' that's who.
> "Who do you think you are?"
>
> An echo – long forgotten
> reverberates, sending me scurrying
> back into my crevasse again...
>
> Who *do* I think I am?
>
> I am who I am – a woman.
> I do not seek your permission
>
> to be who I am.

Sink to the bottom
and there you will find
all the silt and detritus of your life
all the muck and the filth
of your living.

And you can curl up and lie
in the swamp of it
you can become foetus like
in the dark womb
of your doubt.

And then and maybe only
then will you realise that the silt
and the swamp and the darkness
is the seedbed
watered by your tears, fertilized by your despair.

When you are scared
of something
do it anyway.
Why don't you do it afraid?

Do it not knowing
whether you will fail
or succeed.

You do not have to be perfect
just be there.
You do not have to get it right
just be present

If that's how it is
Why don't you do it afraid...?

CREDO 2

When all else fails
I believe in starlings...
When dark reaches
overtake the spilt milk skies
and streaks of red and pink clash noisily
above the heads of stark silhouetted trees

I believe in starlings.
Murmuration.

What to do when there are no waymarks? If this life is truly a journey, a pilgrimage, what is it a journey to, a pilgrimage for? When the tsunami sweeps away the milestones, how does anyone know in which direction to go? When there are no rivers to follow, no mountains to climb, no broken branch, no footprint in the mud to show that someone, something, has passed this way before, do you set your face to the rising sun, or do you walk in the moon's path? Dear one, you will find yourself back where you started and not recognise that is so. Do you follow the wild geese as they migrate north or do you follow the swift and the swallow south? My friend, they will soon out pace you.

When the last pine forest has gone, when the beech trees no longer etch the skyline, how will you know where you are? Will you walk in circles all the sorry days of your life? Or will you take the tattered remnants of your courage in one hand and put your other hand in the hand of the Unknown Mystery and set out? Will you step out without a map – never knowing where you are heading but hoping against hope, certainly or uncertainly, that the Unknown One means you no harm and will walk kindly with you.

Where you are is where you are meant to be.

> Moving beyond the plains of religion
> through the deserts of Christianity and Islam
> with their arid dry sands and illusionary oases
> Beyond the bright tangle of Hindu scrubland
> and all its beauty
> Climbing the foothills of Judaism –
> stumbling and sliding on the dogmatic slippery scree
> Reaching higher climes
> and fresher air of compassionate Sikhism
> and Buddhism...
>
> finally, finally
> when all else is traversed
> and exhausted
> and where mountain top touches
> stratosphere
> where nothing grows
> and nothing is heard
> except the sound of eternity
> and all lays beneath
> and beyond
>
> the buzzard soars.

In the Buddhist tradition of metta, or lovingkindness meditation, you send blessings first to yourself, then your loved ones, then those you are in conflict with, and finally to all beings.

BEYOND RELIGION

beyond dogma and creed,
cult and culture,
beyond learning and knowledge,
rules and rites,
beyond all the faiths
of theism and non-theism...

...there is an ancient land
populated by mountain ranges
where kindness lies
like soft-fallen snow,
where honesty grows tall as pine-trees
in the foothills
where patience blankets the meadows
as waving grasses and
spangled flowers grow,
where forgiveness breathes
as ripples on a cool, still pond,
where compassion and joy
fall like rain into a river
and run laughing to the sea

and love overarches all as does a summer's day sky.

Come with me...

'Love all God's creation, the whole and every grain of sand in it. Love every leaf, every ray of God's light. Love the animals, love the plants, love everything. If you love everything, you will perceive the divine mystery in things. Once you perceive it you will begin to comprehend it better every day. And you will come at last to love the whole world with an all-embracing love.'

FYODOR DOSTOEVSKY.[23]

INTERDEPENDENCE

Do you not yet understand?
We are all one.
Rocks and microbes, viruses
and sunsets
jellyfish and elephants
human beings and flying beings,
bats, wasps, swallows and
vultures
Stateless Refugees, Europeans, Americans, North and South,
Asians, Australasians, Africans
we are all one.
Part of the whole mystery.
Buddhist, Jew, Wiccan,
Muslim, Hindu, Jedi,
God, Allah, Holy Mother,
Grandfather, Krishna, Atheist, Agnostic, Humanist.
All one. And we,
all beings,
are part of the complete mystery.

Now do you understand?

---

[23] Robert Gottfried; Frederick W. Kruger. 'Living in an Icon. 2019

I miss the return of the swallows
and the butterflies on the buddleia.

I miss the bee orchids on the bank
and the violets in the lane.

I miss the cowslips nodding in the breeze
and the jugs of foaming cow parsley.

I miss the murmur of the ewe to her new born lamb
and the haze of bluebells in the woodland.

I miss the fledgling sparrow under the hedge gaping for food
and the lamb races in the early evening – before being called to bed.

Homesick.

Levi Sucre Romero[24]...warns that, "the coronavirus is now telling the world what we have been saying for thousands of years – that if we do not protect biodiversity and nature, then we will face this and worse future threats."[25]

> There will come a time
> when love is the revolution.
>
> Not bombs and guns
> not war
> not rape
> not violence that breeds violence
> not in God's name
> not in the name of Allah.
>
> The biggest
> the most enduring and
> overwhelming revolution will be love
> overcoming all.
> Overcoming power
> and greed
> and status
> and hate
> and dominating religions.
>
> Love will be the revolution.

...poet-farmer Wendell Berry, (who) says, "It may well be that when we no longer know what to do, we have come to our real work,, and when we no longer know which way to go, we have begun our real journey."[26]

> I am thankful Holy One
> that I know a lot less now
> than I knew when I was younger

---

[24] A Bribri indigenous teacher from Costa Rica
[25] Julian of Norwich. Matthew Fox. 2020. p2
[26] Ibid p96

KIVA[27]

As a seed in the deep, dark earth,
slowly, slowly,
surely,
reaches for the light

so my soul, my very self, reaches up from
the dark, dark
places
strengthened and nourished

towards the light.

In the shaded recesses of the earth
the womb, the kiva,
there is a stretching,
a reaching

and a finding.

Time stands still
and rushes on regardless.

Spat out from the whale's belly…
Off I go to Tarsus, dragging my feet.

---

[27] An underground chamber used by Pueblo First Nation people for spiritual ceremonies. Hebrew name meaning SheKnows. Sanskrit name meaning Beautiful, Lotus, Shelter

Why does it matter so much to Richard Dawkins and his ilk that I, and others like me, should believe in that which is called God? It does not matter to me one little bit what Mr Dawkins does or does not believe in. if I am delusionary, what is that to him? Is he trying to save me from myself? And why is he so angry on the subject? I am not angry that he does not believe in God.

His thinking impinges on my thinking only in so much as I am curious as to why he would want to persuade me to his way of thinking and his belief system. I would like to know that. Religion has much to answer for – but then so does Science.

Mystery (do you know that word Mr Dawkins?) is not ignorance or lack of learning, and humility knows that there is not an answer for everything. I am thankful for that. A life where all the questions have been answered would be unutterably dull and uncreative.

Give me your evidence that God does not exist, Mr Dawkins. I think you cannot. You cannot, any more than I can prove God does exist. You and I are linked by a mystery we cannot solve.

'As soon as a mystery is scheduled for solution, it is no longer a mystery; it is a problem'

WENDELL BERRY[28]

[28] Life is a Miracle. 2000. p36

OUTSIDER

Always, the outsider
the one who doesn't belong
longing to... tries, but lacks the camouflage.

Not Italian after all, except for half a nationality.
Greek – who knew?
Not a Christian, whatever that is but a Christ
    follower.

Iberian certainly, Georgian or Spanish
who knew?
Scottish and Scandinavian makes some kind of
    sense.

The hot and cold mingle mongrel-like
Outsider. No country as home, no heritage to claim.
Onwards – to Ithica.

I am an accident of passion
a moment's joy in a drab and war ragged world.
I was not intended to be – becoming
a problem with no solution.
I do not have skeins of ancestor love
weaving me into a tribal tapestry.
Half my ancestors do not know I exist.
No love lost there...
Neither am I to become an ancestor
who dreams into the future of life
and love carried forward.
I am a dead end.

INDIGENOUS

I am indigenous
I belong to a tribe of
just one.
I am a mongrel race.
There is only me in
my tribe.
Only me has
Scottish, Scandinavian,
Iberian, Italian,
Cornish, Greek,
Albanian, Bavarian
and English (and who on earth knows what that is?)
blood running through my veins and sinews and
bones...

...Told you
I am a tribe of one.
There is no one else
to share rituals and worship of ruddy morning sun
or pale-faced moon.
No-one else dances in my circle.
No-one else sings my song with me
To forests and seas...

...There is no loneliness in
my tribe of one.
I am indigenous.
There is a part of me
a cell of mine
in every tribe,
in every dance,
in every song,
in every river,
tree, fish, bird, rock and
mineral.
My tribe is Earth
and that is where I belong...

Indigenous
In my tribe of one.
One Earth.

The truth is
ultimately
we are all of us alone
homesick
for something,
some one
that we will never know
some pinprick of light
a distant star
some far away truth
wrapped in a scroll
buried in a cave
in the arid desert
of our innermost being

> **For everything there is a season, and a time for every matter under heaven.**
> ECCLESIASTES 3

Thank you, Ecclesiastes

A time for birthing a new creation, a time for letting old things die.
A time to plant new ideas and a time to harvest their fruit.
A time to kill hatred of self and a time to heal past wounds.
A time to tear down old protective walls and a time to build anew on their foundations.
A time to cry about what might have been and a time to laugh about what is.
A time to grieve over lost certainties and a time to dance because your soul is breaking free.
A timer to scatter those who dismiss you and a time to gather those who accept and love you for who you are.
A time to use your voice and a time to forget worrying about what others think.
A time to search for meaning and a time to stop looking for simple solutions.
A time to keep the important things and throw away all the window dressing.
A time to tear apart patriarchal theology and a time to mend matriarchal intuition.
A time to love the slow transformation growing inside and a time to hate the rush to have all the answers.
A time for war against resistant structures and governments and a time for justice and peace amid the unholy chaos.

Not here, not there...
everywhere
the world hums with holiness
and the Breath blows
where It will

I invite you, God,
into the pathetic little bit
of stillness that I can muster,
the small bit of space that I can spare.
And you slither in and breathe deeply
and push back my walls
and barriers with a huge grin on your face.
Opportunistic God!

A BLESSING

God bless me with discomfort
at glib answers, superficial friendships
and love treated carelessly.

God bless me with anger
at injustice, the oppression of women
and exploitation of Creation.

God bless me with tears of outrage
at suffering children, war, pornography
and starvation.

God bless me with simplicity and courage
to know that I can do, with you
what cannot be done.

I am further along the journey than I had thought
……but not as far as I had imagined.

Do not live a careful life
Do not avoid being hurt
damaged, even.
Do not shun risk
or slammed doors
Do not be first
to walk away...

Do not keep silent.

Do not hide your light under a bushel
Blaze, blaze,
set your flame on a hill
set alight the beacons...

You have been created
for prophecy and sign
for calming turbulent waters
for rabble-rousing
for walking on water
for trampling on injustice
for lifting the despairing...

Blessed be you
and blessed be your daughters
and blessed be your grandmothers
and blessed be your mothers

and blessed be your womanly soul...

In the end, at the reckoning
I am left with no beliefs.

I cannot believe with any certainty
in a God who created a world in seven days.

I cannot believe with any integrity with
of a virgin giving birth to a saviour.

I cannot believe without question
in a saviour who was killed for me.

I cannot believe in a God
who in the name of Love sends sinners to Hell.

I cannot believe in Heaven where only the elite dwell.

I can try to believe in the unending, eternal story
that I am deeply, deeply loved
and that may be enough for now.

ADDENDUM

January 1st 2025
Another bloody resurrection
another brutal New Year
with its false promises, false starts
and unresolved resolutions.

This time things will be different.
This time I, Life, The World will be better, kinder,
wiser.
This year's wars will cease,
Presidents and Prime Ministers, Governers and
Heads of State
will work for the people, the poor,
the channel-crossers and border hoppers
and not for themselves
and their self-aggrandisement.

This year the Church will shed its finery,
its palaces, its rituals, its gender hang-ups,
its patriarchy
and become the least, the servant
like the Jewish man they pretend to follow.

This year....
Will be just the same as the last bloody year
We have learned nothing.

Acknowledgements with thanks and gratitude...

My grateful thanks go to TM of Mercer Books, without whom this long cherished dream would not have been possible. You took a rank outsider and guided me through this whole book thing when it was patently obvious that I knew nothing. You are a hero!

Much thankfulness goes to my friends, the weavers. To Jackie and Pauline, to Alice and Julie B, and to Corinne who made us laugh and think and taught us to be creative and loving. I have learned so much from you all.

Thank you, Trudi, for the kindness, thoughtfulness and sharing, and all the trips out to places I would never have gone on my own. I am the better for knowing you. Barbara, what can I say? You are a friend through thick and thin and an inspiration with your selfless loving and down to earth commonsense. Thank you for being part of my life.

Thank you, Peter who believed in me, when I didn't. I miss the three hour lunches and wide ranging, sometimes cynical, but always discreet, theological discussions – Norfolk is a long way away. Thank you too, to Iain Mc., Tim R. and Philip H. Your help and insights have been invaluable. Thank you, Ian K. for just being you. I love you the more for it, although I'm still miffed that you won't be doing my funeral...

Thank you too for all those men who put me down, ignored my ideas, patted me on the head and lied to me. Thank you to all the tall men in grey suits. Painful as you have made my life, I have grown because of you. You have shaped who I am. I hope you are proud of yourselves.

The Third Order of Franciscans in Somerset and beyond have given my life focus, even if I don't always follow the rules. They have welcomed me and loved me – even as I have challenged and bewildered them. Thank you, sisters and brothers, for the love and support. Additional thanks must go to Andrew and to Rachael for walking with me and my shortcomings – you are amazing!

Gratitude goes in bucketfuls to The United Reformed Church for nurturing me, training me and widening my horizons. Special thanks go to Stephen T. for his wisdom and patience and creativity.

And then too, thanks must go to the pastorates who were brave enough to take me on as their minister. Wow! I owe you all so much... thank you Paul S. for always supporting me, even when it was difficult for you. Thank you to the good folk of Zion who thought I could be a minister when I did not. Thank you too, Josie C. for all the love, and the gentle manner in which you pointed out the error of my ways. I learned so much from you.

Thank you to Rosie, Jeanne, Marianne and Greg who have nurtured me in body, mind and spirit. And thank you too to Paul D., you have taught me things I never thought I needed to know. Thank you so much Ed for your paintings and creativity and broccoli trees and literary lunches with Melton Mowbray pork pie. You have fed more than my stomach.

Thank you to all the women and men and children who have seasoned my life as a riding instructor, primary teacher, minister and companion on the way – you know who you are and I love you all.

If I've missed anyone, forgive me. You are not forgotten.

Thank you, Julie K, for being such a special part of my life – I love you very much, little sister.

And then there's Richard and Ben and Tom, without whom my life would have no meaning or joy. Thank you for being just the best thing in my world!

Printed in Dunstable, United Kingdom